Reading Clinic
Brain Research Applied to Reading

Reading Clinic

Brain Research Applied to Reading

David Furr, Ph.D.

Truman House Publishing
Chicago

Reading Clinic copyright © 2000 by David L. Furr

Library of Congress Cataloging -in-Publication Data

Furr, David.
    Reading clinic: brain research applied to reading/
    David Furr
        p. cm.
        Includes index.
    ISBN: 0-9700324-0-4
        1. Reading   2. Brain   3. Neuroscience I. Title

Dedicated to
all the parents who trust teachers
and those teachers who never betray that trust
and my wife Pam
and the best kids a parent could hope for
Mike
Jake
Rebecca
Sam

Contents

Acknowledgements

It would be easy to write a few pages acknowledging the help I received with this undertaking. I need to thank Dr. Ed. Mott for convincing me that I could write and Dr. Pat Reynolds for his technical knowledge.

Thanks to Rise Gaines, a truly visionary school principal who inspires me on a regular basis and Ellen Gardner a "real" reading specialist and a good friend.

A special thanks to Robin Young who knew this would work long before I did and to all the wonderful children that I have read with. It was these children who showed me the way.

INTRODUCTION

This book, in many ways, is a miracle. It presents a reading system that has done miraculous things for children. It introduces a new way to teach reading to people, young and old, who have not been able to learn to read using conventional methods. We wrote this book for all the children and all the parents who have shed so many tears over reading difficulties. This book will teach you the same method that we use at Neuro-Learning Systems. We call it "Neuro-Reading". (Pronounced ner row - reading)

If you are reading this book with hopes of finding help for a child under the age of five, you may have the wrong book. This book and the research and program that it presents, is based on the work we have done with children five and older. We have successfully used this method with children as young as 30 months but at this time we have not done that enough times to warrant a discussion. We have no reason to believe that it would not work with younger children but we don't want to present any information that we are not totally sure of. We know that our program will not hurt those under age five, but we feel, at this time, it would be best to investigate other avenues for those children.

Also, please note that our program has not been *proven* to work with children affected by severe autism. We have worked with these children and our program has certainly appeared to work but we have not been able to document this with testing. If you work with children affected by autism you will know how difficult it can be to get reliable test results.

If the previous paragraph does not apply to you, welcome. You are most likely a parent looking for a solution to your child's reading problem. Our studies tell us that we are not the first place you have looked or the first book you have read. You have most likely investigated many avenues and probably not found any that were successful. You have likely spent many dollars and shed many tears. We know your pain and we understand where you are coming from.

We, in this book refers to Neuro-Learning Systems. Neuro-Learning Systems was founded to administer this reading program. This organization professionally administers the program as well as data collection, and research. We have recently (Feb. 2000) finished fine tuning the program (this book reflects those changes) and are engaged in research in methods of teaching math and "teaching" memory. You can contact Neuro-Learning Systems at neuro@read.net or visit our web-site at http://www.neurolearning.net or call 301-253-8979, fax 443-788-2587. We prefer e-mail.

We feel confident in saying that you have finally found a program that will work. Our program has worked for virtually all people with the exception noted earlier. We have been successful at teaching reading to people from age 6 to 55. We believe that it would work for people older than 55 but we have yet to have someone enter our program who was older than 55.

This program works and it works fast. Most of our students are able to advance one grade level per 15 hours of professional tutoring. If you are doing this at home, as opposed to hiring us to tutor, you could get the same results if you are tutoring more frequently. In our studies in preparation for this book, many parents matched or exceeded our results. Most parents took a little longer.

Some students labeled learning disabled in reading were able to shed that label after as little as three months of twice weekly tutoring. This was in our professionally administered program. We think you can do the same at home, if you tutor five or six nights a week, for only 15 or 20 minutes.

We piloted Neuro-Reading with 366 children. There were 183 in our experimental group and 183 in our control group. The majority of them were in special education programs. These initial students were in first through twelfth grade and were either non-readers or two or more grade levels below their current placement. Only three were not successful, all three had been diagnosed with severe autism. We should add that it appeared that even these three learned to read but this could not be confirmed by testing. Our study subjects were representative of most disability groups (no blind or deaf students) and all races were represented.

We present the results of our clinical trials, as well as other data, in more detail on a special page on our website. This is for people who read this book, http://www.neurolearning.net/update You will need to enter this address since it is not published on the site. The data is not included in this book for two reasons, first it is not necessary to know this in order to be successful with this system and two, we tried to write this book as non-technical as possible. We did not want people to get bogged down or turned off with science.

The above is what our system will do. What it will not do is help a third grader read on a sixth grade level. We have found, through research, that our program eliminates deficiencies but it will not create a gifted and talented reader per se. It will bring a child up to their natural ability level. If some deficiency is keeping your third grader from reading on a sixth grade level, this program can help them eliminate that deficiency and consequently read at the advanced level. It cannot make up for plain old experience. Experience is usually what is required for a child to advance in reading levels.

Reading is the foundation of much of learning. Once a student makes it to sixth grade, most learning comes as the direct result of the student's reading. This continues in college. Reading is part of almost every aspect of life. We need to be able to read our mail, directions required to put together a bicycle as well as the reading requirements at work. Without the ability to read, life can be almost impossible. Many times people who do not know how to read will take elaborate measures to hide that fact from those around them. We have had many clients who have told us that they had purchased hundreds of books to display in their homes in the hopes of hiding their reading difficulties from friends and relatives.

We have seen how these methods have transformed lives, not just with reading but also with self-esteem. Most of our clients report remarkable differences in their children. More self-confidence, happier, more full of life, are comments we hear all the time. We are confident that you can see these changes in your child (or adult) as well.

You must follow the system <u>exactly</u>. Glossing over something or skipping something will negate the system. Follow the steps as they are written. You will likely see some promising results your first or second lesson. Do not let that fool you, the first time you decide to skip a lesson or homework will be the "beginning of the end." Next, you will skip a couple of lessons and before you know it, you will be right back where you started.

You should continue to read with your child once the program is finished. Children and adults will begin to backslide if they do not continue to read on a regular basis. We suggest that you continue to read with your child as long as possible (as long as they will let you). Once they read on a fifth or sixth grade level they will be more independent readers. Until they reach that level they will need more intensive support from you. Read at least four nights a week, six nights a week is much better. Remember these are minimums for this system. Whenever you feel that you have had enough, remember the pain that got you here. If you remember the larger pain that your child suffered, you will stay on course.

The vast majority of our students have been eight to thirteen years old. The vast majority were either not able to read anything or reading on a low first grade level. All of these students' school records indicated that they were reading one to two grade levels <u>higher</u> than they actually were. Most of them began this program at a 1.2 or 1.3 reading level. All of them were highly successful. We mention this here because this book may "speak" to that group. If your student is older and/or reading at a higher level, simply make the adjustment in reading levels. Make sure you read our "Advanced User" information if your child is reading above the third grade level. When we say reading, we mean extracting meaning from text, we do not mean simply saying the words with little or no comprehension.

If, while reading this book, you find yourself thinking that this is too simplistic, we ask that you consider two things. First, consider how simplistic learning to speak appears. Next, consider the lesson that the Swiss people learned by not being open to a new paradigm. The Swiss lost 90% of the clock and watch market by being blind to a new paradigm in watches. The way the Swiss had made watches for years blinded them to a new method of watch making. The Japanese took that 90% of the market away from the Swiss because the Swiss refused to look at digital timepieces when its inventor approached them. This is a new paradigm in reading instruction, traditional education would do well by heeding the lessons we have learned.

The State of Reading

More students fail to learn to read by the end of third grade than most people imagine. The National Assessment of Education, a federal government organization, founded in 1994, reported (in 2000) that about forty percent of fourth graders in American schools read below the basic level. This means that these fourth graders were unable to understand "uncomplicated narratives and high-interest informative texts." Even by the time these poor readers graduate from high school, at least thirty percent were still reading below the basic level.

Dr. G. Reid Lyon of the National Institutes of Health (N.I.H.), in an address to congress on April 28, 1998 said that 60 percent of our nation's children have great difficulty learning to read. Further, he stated that about 30 percent of these youngsters will find reading to be the most difficult task that they will have to master throughout their schooling. Dr. Lyon and N.I.H. stated that the psychological, social, and economic consequences of reading failure are legion. It is for that reason that N.I.H. considers reading failure to reflect not only an educational problem, but a significant public health problem as well!

Our nation's efforts to remedy the problem have not been met with great success. Little has changed in the past twenty years. Between 1971 and 1996 the overall pattern of reading achievement has changed minimally. The reading scores of nine and thirteen year olds increased a mere 4 points between 1971 and 1980 but then returned to the former lower levels in 1981. The reading scores of 17-year-olds were about the same in 1996 as they were in 1971. During this same period, the average reading score for white students was higher than those for black and Hispanic students at all three grade levels.

Reading scores do vary somewhat by the type of school and location. On average, students attending private schools consistently scored higher than students attending public schools. In addition, on average, schools located in urban areas generally scored lower than their peers in suburban or rural locations.

Obviously, this is a dismal state of affairs. Given this gloomy report, one would suspect that schools would have somehow solved this issue at least somewhat by now. They have not because the problem is too big and the state of education is too dispersed. In all attempts to "solve" this issue, both public and private schools continue to fight the "phonic wars" instead.

Consider this quote, "The newer demands of daily living on reading, together with scientific research on children and on the reading process have combined to revolutionize reading programs. Many parents of children now in school were taught to read by entirely different methods and accordingly are puzzled by or critical of modern methods." It goes on to say that teachers should attempt to explain the new methods to parents in order to placate them. This quote is found in "Children Learn To Read" a textbook for teachers published in 1947!

Book Chapters

Chapter two of this book explains the research and studies behind this system. It also discusses reading in general and the difficulties of most public schools' reading programs. Chapter 2 can give you some good background information so it is worthwhile reading. Chapter 3 is an overview of the reading process. Chapter 4 is where we begin our explanation of how to implement this program. Chapter 4 shows the specific procedures to use in your reading program. Chapter 5 contains information of special interest to teachers. Chapter

6 discusses case studies. Within these case studies, you can see where this program has been most successful as well as noting things to watch for. The final chapter sums up the program and provides additional advice. Following these chapters are four appendixes that contain tests, lists of words, and other useful information that you will need in order to use this program.

BRAIN RESEARCH AND "NEURO-READING" DEVELOPMENT
Development of the Neuro-Reading Method

As with most "great discoveries," this one came by accident. It took years to recognize. I began to realize that there was something unusual about reading when I was a student at the Defense Language Institute (D.L.I.) in Monterey, California. I had recently joined the U.S. Army and was assigned for training as a Russian Intelligence Analyst. It was at D.L.I. that I began to look at the English language. I quickly realized that I actually knew very little about English grammar. I had always been a very good reader and had never had the occasion to examine my grammar skills. Since they teach Russian by referring to its English counterparts, D.L.I. quickly became a serious challenge. It required that I learn English grammar in order to apply what I was learning about Russian grammar.

Something else happened at Russian school to prepare me for a careful examination of the English language. I managed to learn Russian quite well yet I never ever learned the names of the Russian letters. I did not even know this until years later when I went to work for the National Security Agency. I asked a fellow employee about a military unit known as B Company. When I said the Russian for B Company, my co-worker informed me that I was not saying B but instead I was saying the phonetic sound for B. I had no idea! How could I ever have learned enough about the Russian language to be able to read, write, and speak on an advanced level but not have learned the "A, B, C's"?

Years later, I became a teacher, an elementary school teacher. The schooling I received glossed over phonics, assuming that I was already accomplished in this area. When I applied for a job, and later began teaching no one ever tested or asked me about my ability to teach phonics. It was only when someone asked me to teach phonics did I realize how poor my knowledge of the subject was. I then set out to learn phonics seriously. Since I had always been an excellent reader, I had assumed that at least I knew the basics. The basics, it turned out, was all I knew. I was surprised to find out that there was a soft and hard "g". When I looked at words with a soft g and words with a hard g, I knew how to pronounce them perfectly. How could that be? Had I learned the phonics skills and not the name of the skills? No, the simple fact was that I had not learned all of the skills, per se, but somehow had found a way to pronounce words correctly. I found that I could not distinguish between the soft sounds for "e" and "i." Long sounds I knew well.

What did this mean? I had no idea and did not ask anyone. I set out to learn phonics well and I did. I now know and feel comfortable with all of the phonics rules. This skill came AFTER I had received my second master's degree. I never gave it a lot of thought until after I received a Ph.D., and began to wonder how I had become such a good reader with such poor phonics skills. I especially wondered about that when I was attempting to teach reading to children in special education programs. Every teacher in every program I came across approached the teaching of reading as a phonics task. Children who can not read are asked to learn more phonics. I would feel so sorry for kids who must have heard the same boring stuff repeatedly. No wonder school turned them off.

As the years went by and real student successes were rare, I really began to feel the student's pain. What do you say to yourself when you cannot do something that most people find easy? Do you just write it off as you are stupid and you cannot help it? Although I came across many students who appeared to have given up, I found that all but a very few were willing to set down one-on-one with you. They just were not letting go of the hope. After five, six, seven, years of trying with little or no success, these kids were ready willing and able to try just one more method.

The only method that I ever tried that had at least some small measure of success was the Neurological Impress Method. Interestingly, when I mentioned this method to most teachers they had either not heard of it or dismissed it as not worthwhile. The Neurological Impress Method was developed after World War II to help soldiers who had sustained serious head injury. It is a method where the teacher reads almost directly into a student's ear while the student attempts to read the same material at the same time. I did not have tremendous success with this method but I was able to make small gains with some students. It was this method, however, that made me look in directions different from what I had learned at school.

Another set of circumstances forced me to look at the method of teaching reading that is offered in the majority of schools in America. While working at a middle school in Maryland, I began to examine the ways and means of administering all instruction. The methods employed by most of the teachers at this school seemed to me to be almost abusive. Teachers would stand in front of the class and talk, they would demand that everyone be quiet. After they talked about a subject for forty minutes, they would ask if anyone had a question. If students asked a question, teachers often accused them of "not paying attention."

Somehow, talking about a subject was teaching the subject. There would be 28 students of varying abilities in these classes. Teachers taught the lesson one way and at one ability level; making no attempt to compensate for individual differences. Students who did not understand would be classified as those that didn't care or didn't pay attention. This was at a school that had three excellent principals. These principals worked very hard and tried to change teacher attitudes but were not successful for the most part. I discovered that principals are limited in what they can do with poor employees.

There are many good teachers in America's schools. I taught in four very large school systems and met a few whom I would describe as consistently excellent every day. These teachers understood that you had to teach children, not just lecture at them. If these teachers taught a lesson and half the class did not understand, they would re-teach the lesson, not blame half the class for not paying attention. They also understood that part of their job was motivating students. At least part of the job of motivating students is making the instruction interesting to students, this is no small task.

I believe that most teachers do not understand this and of those that do few know how to accomplish this. I also believe that this is not really the teacher's fault. It is the fault of the school system administrators who run teacher education programs. They almost never offer training in motivation or even the psychology of learning. The excellent teachers that I observed are wonderful teachers not because of their college training but because of their intelligence, nature, and their respect for all people, even little people.

So, if lecturing does not always work, what does work? I found that average and above average students could usually "get by" with lecture. They were smart enough to either, understand what was said, or know what questions to ask to help them understand. Other children flounder in a lecture environment. I looked at what was not working and investigated what did work. The only two "things' that I ever witnessed consistently working were the way children were taught to speak (by their mothers) and the way they learned to play Nintendo! As I seriously looked into how we learn to speak as well as how children become accomplished at Nintendo, I quickly discovered that each method shared common elements.

The common elements are "sugar coating" and repetition. These two elements, when combined with "modeling" are the brains best ways of learning. Although we are just beginning to

15

understand the brain, we do know certain things. What we do know, which is discussed later, supports these three ingredients to learning. When compared to traditional methods of teaching reading, it is easy to understand why we have had a ninety-nine percent success rate and why traditional education has had a sixty-three percent success rate.

Briefly, traditional education teaches children about the alphabet, phonic sounds, and sight words. We expect children to take this knowledge and apply it to the task of reading. They also get to hear their teacher read, while he or she sits at the front of the room.

At the age of five or six, children are expected to make the mental leap to application. When they experience difficulties, they are taught "reading strategies" or things to do when you do not know a word. They learn to guess based on the pictures or content. Not many first or second graders understand either. Recent research says that the average child is wrong in those guesses eighty-nine percent of the time. (Baldwin & Schatz 1985, Gough & Hillinger 1980, Juel, Griffith, & Gough 1986, Nicholson 1991, Schatz & Baldwin 1986, Schwantes, Boesl, & Ritz 1980, Share & Stanovich 1995, Smith 1994, Stanovich 1991) Adults do much better, because they have much finer tuned reasoning skills and have had significant life experience. The studies that were used to verify the validity of teaching context clues were all done with high school students. High school age students probably have a little too much life experience, whereas seven year olds do not.

After looking at reading instruction with a fresh perspective, I do not find it amazing that schools do so poorly in teaching children to read. I find it amazing that they do as well as they do. It seems like such a difficult way to learn something. Yet the vast majority of schools use the same method with small differences.

In our program at Neuro-Learning Systems, the first thing we tell children (and adults) is that they do NOT have to sound out words. Every student, young and old, heave a giant sigh of relief. This one thing, if nothing else, tends to motivate students to do well. Note: Our students sound out words towards the middle or end of our program, after they are accomplished readers of lower level material.

When compared to the traditional method of teaching reading and the success or failure of these methods it becomes exceedingly clear that our method is far superior. Our success rate and the findings of current brain research provide us with a clear picture of what works and what doesn't work.

Brain Research

President Bush (George W.'s father) declared the nineties as the decade of the brain. The nineties, especially the late nineties, witnessed a tremendous surge in brain research. Some of the findings are preliminary in nature, in that their application will only come as the result of more research. For example, in 1999 we found that the brain can generate new cells. This neuro-genesis is the opposite of what was the standard belief of most, if not all, well known and respected brain researchers. Simply knowing that this is possible is not of particular help but it does open new and incredibly large doors to new learning and new applications.

Brain research in the last few years has yielded many interesting things that we can apply to education. Many of these findings require little effort to implement. Most could have a huge impact on education.

The Learning Brain

We know a lot about how the brain works. We know that learning and memory are tied to the neurons in the brain and the interconnections that these neurons make. The average brain has from ten to one hundred billion neurons. Each neuron makes about one thousand connections to other neurons. Neurons form neural networks that are the biological basis of learning.

The typical neuron consists of a cell body; a tentacle like fiber called an axon, which transmits outgoing information to other neurons and a dendrite. The axon can connect directly to another neuron's cell body or, more often, to another cell's dendrite. The dendrite acts as the receptor of information from other neurons. A dendrite is shaped like a tree with numerous branches. Each dendrite can have hundreds of branches that can grow to form thousands of connections.

We call the connection between a dendrite and an axon a synapse. Researcher G.M. Shepard says that there are sixty trillion synapses in the typical brain. Synapses are critical to brain function and memory. The actual physical "connection" is not actually a connection at all. There is a gap between the axon and dendrite that is approximately one five thousandth of a millimeter. The latest research reports that there are synapses that have no gap at all and in them there is a direct electrical transmission of information. In the more typical synapse, a bioelectrical impulse travels down the axon at speeds (conduction velocity) from 1.2 to 250 miles per hour. It stops at the end causing a neurotransmitter, a chemical, to release in the gap. This chemical carries the "message" across the synapse and into the dendrite.

A healthy neuron can make thousands of intricate connections with other neurons. A typical neuron will have from one to a thousand synapses. These connections can be as short as a micrometer or as long as the distance from the brain to the base of the spinal column. The actual mechanism is far more complex than described above but this should suffice for our purposes.

The key to the message's success is the connection and the neurotransmitters. These connections play a role in every aspect of our behavior. Scientists believe that this is "memory in the making." When new learning takes place, new neural connections are made. The more the neural pathway is used the stronger and larger it becomes. In this case, bigger is definitely better. The brain prunes smaller, unused, neural pathways.

Amino acids make neurotransmitters from the protein foods you eat. The body's proteins make twenty-two amino acids. Amino acids manufacture fifty thousand proteins that your body needs. It is a simple matter to consume the necessary proteins that supply healthy brain chemicals.

Your body can produce all the brain chemicals it needs when you consume "complete proteins" such as fish, fowl, eggs, meat, cheese and yogurt. Eating "incomplete proteins", your body can obtain some of the necessary proteins for what it needs. Incomplete proteins are grains, nuts, seeds, and leafy green vegetables. Adequate nutrition is imperative to maintaining optimal brain health. Food is definitely your best way to maintain proper chemistry. The delicate balance is far too complex to attempt to manipulate with amino acid supplements.

Reading Problem Theory

Marcel Proust said, "The real voyage of discovery consists not in seeking new landscapes but in having new eyes." It is with "new eyes" that we looked at reading. It is our hypothesis that neural networks are not only the keys to learning but also hold the key to understanding reading problems. We believe that children who are having reading difficulties have formed neural pathways that are incorrect. Incorrect in that they are formed with inaccurate information. For example, when a child has not learned from the more traditional method of teaching reading, by putting together sounds, they are confronted with words that have no meaning to them. When a young child is presented with the word "because" and does not know it, his or her teacher asks him to "sound it out." If the child does not understand how to do this, the child attempts to please the teacher by making a guess. The problem is the guess. Guessing that "because" is the word "better" the child has set into motion the development of neural connections that will enable him to recognize this word again at a later time.

We now arrive at that later time. The child sees the word "because" but this time either someone else says the word or the child is told that the word is "because." Another neural network forms connecting the letters b-e-c-a-u-s-e with the brain's understanding of "because". Now we have two neural networks for one word. These neural networks are tenuous at best and the next time a child observes "because" he or she may say "because" or "better" or something else that seems (to the child) appropriate. We have seen numerous cases where "because" could be stated as "ride," "color," "look," or "people" or any other incorrect word. If you watch a child look at a word they do not know and they have been having reading problems, they actually appear uneasy or unsettled. No doubt the brain is unsettled as well.

Using this knowledge and the knowledge of "pruning," we have been able to help children correct this problem. Pruning takes place when the brain re-absorbs or discards neural connections. We have all experienced this. You can learn a foreign language and become an accomplished speaker. Discontinue using the foreign language on a regular basis and you will be surprised at how rapid it is lost. The key to the loss is the scarcity of use of the neural networks.

This makes a lot of sense for reasons you probably never considered. Your brain takes in a lot of information. Take for example a visit to a restaurant with a friend. As you enter the restaurant, you access prior learning by looking for the hostess. (If not for prior learning you would not know there would be a hostess.) As the hostess seats you, you notice an area in the rear of the restaurant that is, most likely, where the restrooms are located. While you wait for your friend to arrive, you look over the menu and read about foods that you have never examined. You select and reject based on previous learning. You notice that the person seated next to you is wearing a perfume that your mother wears and you remember that you have to call her. Your friend arrives and you discuss business, trying to come up with novel ways to approach old problems. You eat while you are talking and take in numerous sights and aromas. You pay the bill and remember to pay another bill at home that is over due. This restaurant has been okay but you probably will not return any time soon.

All of these experiences, and thousands more not noted, enter your brain. For perception and understanding to take place neural connections must be made. New connections are formed, about the comfort of the chair you sat in, as well as the connections that attach to prior learning, like the fact that most restaurant rest rooms are in the rear of the building.

Some of these connections are frivolous, like the comfort of the seat, others are not so frivolous, like where the rest rooms are, and some are very important such as the solution you found for the business problem. If the brain accumulated and stored all of these sensations, textures, colors, etc., your brain would probably be full in a week. The brain, to survive and be useful, must prune most of these connections.

The brain prunes the connections, most often, simply based on use or lack of use. If you never consider the comfort of that particular chair again, you will most likely forget it. If you do not practice conjugation of verbs in the Russian you learned you will lose that as well.

Neuro-Reading takes advantage of this pruning and the ability of the brain to form correct neural pathways or the brain's "plasticity" as it is sometimes called. By focusing on words that have just previously been spoken for the student, we think we promote the creation of a shortcut to learning that word. We also prevent the student from forming incorrect neural networks by giving them the pronunciation of the word. We prevent more incorrect connections from forming and we reduce the reinforcement of the previously constructed (bad) networks. By telling the student the correct word before they guess a wrong word, and thus creating another bad pathway, we help build bigger correct pathways and speed the pruning of the incorrect paths.

The texts that we use with lower level readers are texts that use the "high frequency" words so common in language. They use the words most frequently used in reading and writing over and over again. This repetition forms stronger, thicker neural pathways. Most readers are not even aware of the repetition because the words appear in different stories. This is a decisive factor of this system. There are other components but those discussed in the last few pages are the most important.

While in the process of experimenting with this system, we had an idea. Our idea, based on our observations and successes, was that the difference between a child reading alone, and a child strongly concentrating on the words while an adult read were not very dissimilar. We believed that the brain processes involved would have to be similar.

We tested our hypothesis by taking images of the brain while reading and taking other images of the brain while the student, following with his finger, listened to someone else read. The images were not exact but it was obvious that most of the same processes were involved. The images were very similar. If you saw them side by side, you would probably not see a difference. Only when superimposed can you detect a slight difference. Noticing this reinforced what we were already doing with students. In a very unscientific method, we asked children to read something silently (on their ability level) and took a picture of their brain. We then asked the same child to follow along while an adult read something above their ability level. We again took a picture, the pictures were very close to identical.

If further research finds these initial assumptions to be correct, reading and learning to read could see more dramatic changes. We hope to expand this research as time and funding permit.

Some of the other components of this system as it relates to brain research are found below.

Natural Light

A recent study has shown that students in classrooms where there is more natural daylight progress up to twenty-five percent faster on standardized tests than students in classrooms without natural daylight. We recommend that our students do their lessons in as much natural daylight as possible. Natural light contains the full range of the visible spectrum and is much more restful on the eye. Artificial lights give off a very narrow band of light wavelengths or an unbalanced light spectrum. These wavelengths cause undue strain on the eye especially in certain cells of the retina.

In most of today's classrooms, the shades are drawn and artificial lights are burning. Not only is this inadvisable it is also wasteful of natural resources. Classrooms usually contain the fluorescent lighting that emits the narrow band of wavelengths mentioned above. In many schools there are no windows and therefore no choice when it comes to lighting.

Visual Guides

Using the finger as a visual guide is important to our program. This is true for two reasons. Many of the students in our program have had "visual tracking" problems. They have difficulty staying on track with the words and sometimes lose their place when trying to move down to the next line. Using the finger as a guide not only helps the person stay on track, we have found that it appears to actually fix the problem if the student uses their finger for four or more months. It also helps the student stay focused and maybe even extend the amount of time that the student looks at a word. It is critical to the success of our program.

Brain research into using visual guides has determined that there are other benefits as well. In one study it was shown that students using a visual guide increased their reading speeds by more than fifty percent. A visual guide can help reduce or eliminate back-skipping. It can also help speed up the eye when the student purposely moves his or her finger faster.

Nutrition

Recent brain research tells us that what a person eats is not only important but also critical. We have known for years that we cannot concentrate on learning if we are hungry. This is one of the reasons schools serve free meals, including breakfast, to children who parents claim poverty. We have always known that it is important for children to eat a balanced and nutritious diet but now we also know that the poor intake of vitamins and minerals can dramatically affect the inner workings of the brain. Numerous research studies have pointed out that children of poverty are almost always at the bottom of the learning totem pole.

In the last few years, we have learned that the brain uses glucose (sugar) as it learns. In one study, children who drank a glass of juice before each lesson or test in a particular subject did thirty-three percent better than a control group. We advise our students to drink a glass of juice, which raises the blood sugar level rapidly, before each reading lesson. We must also be careful because the consumption of large amounts of sugar can cause many health problems. Further, brain research tells us that those diets high in saturated fats and sugar can impede learning.

We also know that neurotransmitters are the crux of the proper operation of the brain. What we eat is directly related to the levels of neurotransmitters in our body. Without the proper food, the body is just not able to use amino acids to build the necessary neurotransmitters. Without these numerous types of neurotransmitters, the brain cannot operate in the full range that is possible.

We have to be careful here. We are not advising you to load your children up with sugar. First, the body can make glucose (sugar) from carbohydrates and second, a large amount of sugar in one's diet can cause serious health problems like diabetes. The best advice is to watch your child's diet and make sure they eat sensibly. Unless they are diabetic, we recommend the juice for our lessons. A small glass of juice has other good nutrients as well as the ability to raise blood glucose levels rapidly.

Posture

It is important to read and study at a table. A kitchen type table and chair are best. Lying on a bed or floor is worst. Slouched in a chair may seem comfortable but it is anything but good for your brain and spinal cord. A firm chair that allows your thigh to be horizontal and your calf to be at a right angle to the thigh is best. Press your lower back against the chair. Your upper back should lean slightly towards the book you are reading. In this position, your nervous system can operate at optimal speed and your muscles should not become tired.

Associations

We also know that the brain learns quicker and remembers better the broader our knowledge is of a particular subject. The brain is also a natural compiler and organizer of information. That is what it does best. In one study, people who knew more about the rules and methods of baseball were able to memorize a simple list of baseball scores fifty times better than those who knew little about the subject.

What we now know is that the physical connections that the brain makes during learning, the neural networks, actually grow thicker when you obtain supplemental knowledge. The thicker the neural network the better and longer the retention of knowledge. We also know the opposite; that simple rote learning of isolated facts forms very thin neural networks that usually prune themselves rather quickly.

How can we apply this new knowledge to learning? Although it is simple, it is not often used. The way public school systems are set up can impede this from occurring. It is what teachers call teaching with "thematic units." That simply means that teachers take a topic, let us say Japan, and they read about Japan, do math related to Japan, art projects about Japan, even play Japanese games in physical education class. They do not do this just to learn about Japan; when they are reading about Japan, they are learning to read as well as learn about Japan. Japan becomes the glue to hold things together. You can use almost anything: football, motorcycles, anything that you can relate to music, art, reading, math, etc.

Why don't most schools do this? That is a good question; unfortunately, the answer is not very pretty. We asked two hundred teachers why they do not use thematic units. Most agreed that thematic units foster learning but for the most part, teachers think that the coordination of such ventures is too difficult. They also do not want to give up any autonomy. We have seen this work in schools where the overriding concern was student learning, not commiseration for teachers.

Temperature

Brain research also tells us that room temperature is important. Optimal room temperature for the brain is 65 degrees Fahrenheit (18 Celsius). The brain operates best at this temperature. If you can control the temperature certainly you should. Recent studies show that an increase in temperature of ten degrees decreases optimal brain functioning by fifteen percent. As the temperature rises brain function decreases. The study did not investigate the effect of very cold temperatures. If you have ever worked or studied in a non-air-conditioned brick building you all ready know that this is true. It is obvious even to the casual observer that everything, including people and time, slow in sweltering buildings.

Study or Reading Time

Recent research appears to suggest that studying or reading during the same time period and in the same physical environment is beneficial. The best time of day appears to be dependent on an individual's habits.

Regardless of the setting and time, the study session should contain certain elements in regards to timing. The beginning and the end of a lesson is remembered best in all learning situations. We know this as primacy and recency. We remember the beginning and the end better as we do any outstanding items. With this in mind, coupled with the limits of attention span, we know it is best to study or read in forty-minute increments. Five to ten minute breaks every forty minutes are well worth the time if used properly.

Break time should be used to rest, relax the eyes and stretch. Taking regular breaks can actually maximize learning time. Breaks allow the brain to fully use the primacy and "recency" phenomena. Even if reading seems to be going great, it is still advisable to take a short break.

Attitude and Emotion

One of the things that you will read a lot about in this book is attitude. There is a reason for this. It is most likely the single most important ingredient in this and all educational endeavors. This is not just an opinion, recent brain research supports this claim.

Brain researchers have determined that emotion actually causes physical changes in the brain. When we are unhappy or stressed our brain produces a chemical that actually destroys some of itself. The area it destroys is largely responsible for memory.

The primary area of your brain that deals with

stress is the limbic system. Its has an enormous influence on emotions and memory. Whenever you perceive a threat, real or imagined, a car crash or fear of a teacher, the limbic system immediately responds via your autonomic nervous system. This elaborate network of endocrine glands automatically regulates your metabolism. It has two paths or branches, each working in opposing directions.

The hormones that act as chemical messengers travel through your bloodstream to accelerate or suppress metabolic functions. The trouble is that certain stress hormones do not know when to quit working in opposite directions. They remain active in your brain far too long, injuring and even destroying the brain cells you need for memory and learning. With your body and mind in this temporary state of metabolic overdrive, you are now prepared to respond to a life-threatening situation. The only problem is that stress is most often not life threatening. As the stress goes away, your body tries to return to normal. This, however, may not happen so easily.

Although the nervous system jumps into action immediately, it is very slow to turn off and allow the tranquilizing parasympathetic nervous system to take over and calm you down. Once the stress response has begun, the system keeps you in a state of high readiness.

We experience many problems, or stresses, that our brain perceives as life threatening, although they are clearly not. The thought of a failing grade or mortgage payment does not need an intense physical response, but we get one anyway. Chronic overreaction to stressors overloads us with powerful hormones that are only intended for short-term activation in emergency situations. These are especially harmful to children who are still developing. The earlier you insult a body system, the heavier the toll.

The cumulative effect damages and kills brain cells. Too many stress hormones can prevent the brain from forming a new memory. Stress hormones can damage the very part of the brain that's supposed to signal when to shut-off their production — creating a vicious cycle that destroys parts of the brain and can even diminish the quality of life.

The renowned brain researcher, Robert M. Sapolsky, has shown that sustained stress can damage the hippocampus, the part of our limbic brain that is central to learning and memory. The reason this happens is due to "glucocorticoids," a class of steroid hormones secreted from the adrenal glands during stress. They are more commonly referred to as cortisol.

In addition, during a perceived threat, your adrenal glands immediately release adrenaline. After a couple of minutes, if the threat is severe or persists, the adrenals then release cortisol. Once in the brain, cortisol remains active much longer than adrenalin and continues to affect brain cells.

Chronic over secretion of cortisol adversely affects brain function, especially memory. Human studies show a correlation between high cortisol levels, decreased memory, and cognitive functions like concentration.

First, because stress hormones divert blood glucose to exercising muscles, the amount of glucose that reaches the hippocampus is less than normal. This creates a situation in the hippocampus that makes it unable to create new memories.

Cortisol also interferes with the function of neurotransmitters, the chemicals that brain cells use to communicate with each other. This makes it difficult to think or access long-term memories.

So what does this have to do with reading? We have found that 100 percent of children who are experiencing reading problems are also under a lot of stress. Their stress is often directly related to reading. Their parents or teachers activate the stress simply by asking them to read. This coupled with the requirements of school can produce a high state of stress. In children it is sometimes difficult to see but it is there performing its destruction.

Stress is an interesting phenomenon. The person experiencing the stress solely determines its definition. It does not matter one bit how frivolous or inappropriate you think that stress generator is. It only matters what the person experiencing the stress thinks.

Like adding insult to injury, a recent study released in July 1999, found that when you suppress emotion you redirect neurological resources away from memory processing. Researchers Richards and Gross found that emotional suppression has its costs. No one who hides their emotions should be in a learning environment because short-term memory is short-circuited when someone is expending the energy required to hide emotions.

How many children in school do you think this affects? How many children feel unjustly treated, rightly or wrongly? We have never heard of any incidents when a child was denied recess or screamed at and that child said, "Oh well, I had it coming, I really did know better".

Priming

Priming is, relatively speaking, a newly discovered phenomenon. It refers to an improved ability to process, detect, or identify a word or other stimulus, after having recently been exposed to the word. Many researchers, Larry Squire, David Mitchell and many others are currently looking at this unusual ability.

Priming may be a totally separate form of memory. It is thought to be highly visual and that it occurs early in the visual processing pathways even before the analysis of meaning. It appears that information presented this way, as is done with Neuro-Reading, may be stored in the posterior cortex where it allows words to be processed more efficiently. Priming is an exciting area currently under study. There is a good discussion of it in Memory: From Mind to Molecules, a super book by Squire and Kandel.

OVERVIEW OF THE METHOD

The best way to explain this particular method is to think of it in the same terms as when you learned to speak. If you do not remember how it happened and if you are not a parent yourself, think about it. The way we learned to speak and this reading method share three things. They both use modeling, repetition, and tons of positive attitude and expectations. If you ever get to a point in this program where you have a question or unusual circumstance, think about the way you either learned to speak or the way you taught your child to speak. Then apply those principles.

We learned to speak only after hearing others speak a great deal. Next, someone, most likely your mom, cuddled and snuggled you and said, "Say 'mom'." She probably said this many, many times. She also smiled and kissed you and asked you to make a sound that was within your capability. She did not say, "Say encyclopedia." There was never a thought that you would fail, and you did not. You had tons of modeling, repetition, and a super attitude. That is exactly the way we designed this program.

For you cynics out there who might say that learning to speak is a natural process and therefore not comparable. Recent research has shown that learning to speak is not "hard wired." In November of 1970, a famous case illustrated this point. There was a very unfortunate child born to parents who saw her as a nuisance. They never spoke to her or interacted with her. They kept Genie tied to a potty-chair in a small bedroom providing her only with food. This nightmare went on for over ten years.

When social workers finally found this poor child she was unable to speak and had many obvious problems. Even her distance vision was limited to the size of the room.

They took the girl to the University of California at Los Angeles so that she could receive the "best" of care and instruction. After many years of trying, Genie was able to learn many words and was able to convey her meaning but she could not seem to learn grammar or syntax. Many things were learned in this "experiment". First, if humans were born with the ability to speak, why couldn't she? This and other tragic stories have disproved the "natural language" theories.

The "Wild Boy of Aveyron" or "Kamala, the Wolf Girl" are other examples like the one above. They all learned locomotion, but none developed a complex form of communication. Language, in various forms, is universal, but it is one of the most variable of all human institutions.

Modeling, repetition, and attitude are the keys to Neuro-Reading. Let us look at the three components individually, the most important first. Attitude is tantamount to success, a great attitude can overcome almost anything, and a bad attitude can destroy even Herculean efforts. Every good teacher we have ever met had a great attitude and every poor teacher we have ever met had a bad attitude, no exceptions! Who would want to do anything if they are expected to fail at it? Everyone we ever knew in high school loved the subjects that they got good grades in. Or, is it that they got good grades in the subjects they loved? Most likely, it was both!

Every adult on the planet has had at least one success and one failure. If you truly examine those successes and failures, you will find that the failures are fueled, at least in part, by halfhearted attempts and/or less than great attitudes. If you are a child, these "rules" not only apply, they are magnified. Do not be misled by failures that are way beyond your means. Not everyone can be a great athlete like Cal Ripkin Jr., but as Cal Ripkin Jr. will tell you, everyone can learn to read. (Cal and his wife Kelly, donate thousands of dollars annually to reading programs.)

Starting children where they "are," not where their age or grade suggests they should be is a hallmark of Neuro-Reading. This issue, of teaching students at the appropriate level, is intensely important. It certainly is a pillar of our program but it is probably the main reason that children fail at school. Children go to school based on age. For the vast majority, everything they do in school is based on their age. Every teacher and parent in the world knows that all children are different. Some walk at nine months, others at nineteen months. Some learn to speak clearly at twenty months, others at forty months. To think that every child is ready to learn to read at age five is silly and our schools are set up to teach in just this fashion.

Ready or not, at age five, children are taught reading. Those that are not ready become bored and lost. Even worse, they are treated much the same whether or not they actually learn anything. We promote them to the next grade because, until the late 1990's, most educators felt that this was the best thing to do. In most school systems, it is rather difficult to retain a student. More recent studies, one done at Johns Hopkins University, suggest that retention in the primary grades is not such a bad idea after all.

Students later find themselves in first or second grade and they are now actually mature enough to begin to learn to read. We treat these "beginners" as if they were intermediate readers. The children are now ready for lesson number one or maybe two, we offer them lesson number sixty-seven! Since many of the other children are doing just fine with lesson number sixty-seven, these children are out in the cold. What do you do in first grade if you do not understand what is going on? Has anyone ever heard a first grader say, "Excuse me, but it seems as if I have missed something here. Can you fill me in?" Not likely! They do not know enough to say that. What they do is sit quietly, because they know that sitting quietly is important! Parents and teachers hope these students will finally "get it" but how can they. By the time everyone agrees they might be having problems that are not just "not paying attention", everyone else is on lesson eighty-seven!

At a teacher's meeting I attended, the principal asked the fifty or so teachers in attendance if they knew what to do when they discovered that a child was very far behind in reading. One other teacher (who was retiring the next week) and I raised our hands. If teachers do not know what to do, what do they do? Most often they "refer" the child for testing or they do nothing. When these children realize what is going on and how far behind they are they usually become a behavior problem. From that point on they are known as a behavior problem. Teachers say that they could read better if they would just behave properly. We have seen these behaviors disappear when children complete our program. Almost over night, these children see themselves in a better light. We have many parents that believe that not only do these things change but that their child's actual appearance changes. They walk with their heads higher and have happier faces.

This brings us back to attitude. If you are an adult and you are going to use this program with a child, you are in charge of attitude, not the child. The child has plenty of reasons and excuses why he or she may have a less than perfect attitude. You have to take control of this territory. You must set the tone and the manner in which you handle this very worthwhile and critical task.

Most parents are worried, they have seen so much failure that they are worried they will see it again. Parents have to rise above this. You must take charge and be the head cheerleader as well as the principal motivator. As you move through the program, your child's success will serve as a great motivator for both of you. You must approach a task as one that will succeed! Period! No ands, ifs, or buts. This is going to work.

All you have to do is follow simple directions. Approach it any other way and you are wasting your time and hurting your child. In all of your thoughts and communications, you must act as if success is a foregone conclusion. Do not allow yourself to think thoughts such as, "What will we do if this doesn't work?" Instead, think thoughts like, what kind of books will my child develop an interest in, what will my child decide to major in when he or she goes to college. These are real thoughts, necessary thoughts. If you cannot operate in this manner, do not begin, you would be doing more harm than good.

The Reading Process

Language is based on symbols and conventions. If we observe something with four legs, a back, and a seat to sit on, we call this a "chair" because that is the conventional thing to do. We could, however, call this same object a "horse" if everyone agreed that this thing would be called a "horse". Similarly, there is absolutely no reason at all why the symbol "S" should stand for the hissing sound that we commonly ascribe to it. We have simply adopted these symbols or groups of symbols to represent these objects and these sounds. A chair is represented by the letters c.h.a.i.r and the sound those letters represent together only because people have agreed that these are suitable representations.

The fact that language is based on symbols and conventions causes important educational implications. These conventions necessitate that our children understand that one group of symbols represent "money" while another represents "mommy". It is important that children say mommy instead of money when referring to their mother.

Not only must we teach our children to use the correct symbols but they must also be able to recognize the reality behind the symbols of others. Typically, children develop meaning associated with symbols or groups of symbols slowly. They usually develop a less complex association and then add to it. The word chair probably first means the chair that the particular child sits in. Later the larger chairs that adults sit in come to be understood as chairs. Gradually the child will see that chairs have certain characteristics and common elements. Then the idea of chair has taken on supplementary and more complex meaning.

This process of expanding meaning to encompass "different" objects as related to each other is only one of the difficult tasks of language. Adding meaning to more abstract words such as "fairness" and "freedom" can be a lengthy and troublesome process for children. When considering these concepts it becomes obvious that language is not a natural activity. Reading, as part of language, is considerably more complex and less natural. Some languages, like English, have symbols that represent sounds while others, like Chinese, have symbols that represent pictures.

All learners go through a "process" in the course of learning to read English, regardless of the method they use. The following is not a look at our program, it is a look at the general process of reading in English.

The reading process involves the following steps:

1. Perceptual processing
2. Word recognition
3. Syntactic processing
4. Semantic processing
5. Comprehension

Perceptual Processes

We know that perceptual processes develop before birth. Perceptual processes are those processes that include the ability to translate sound and light into information that we can understand and make use of. Assuming that the visual and auditory systems develop normally, the processes, as we believe, are as follows:

The eyes contain what are known as rods and cones. It is here in the rods and cones that visual perceptual processing actually begins. There are about six million cones and one hundred twenty million rods in the fovea or center of the eye. Situated in the center of the retina, the fovea is about 1.5 mm in diameter. It is in the fovea that light comes in contact with the cones and rods and is converted into signals that are electrical in nature. The brain then processes these electrical signals. On the fringe of the fovea is the parafovea. We use both fovea and parafovea in the process of reading.

Word Recognition

How children attempt to recognize words is determined to a large degree by how they are trained to recognize words. Typically children are taught in kindergarten and first grade to identify individual graphemes and transform these to the sounds that they represent. At the same time they are introduced to words known as "sight words," words that do not always conform to phonic rules and/or are words that are used so often they must be identified instantly. Words such as the, this, a, what, etc. fall into this category. At the same time children are learning this, they are also learning letter and word shapes that will aide them in sight word recognition as well as general word recognition. Beyond that, no one really knows for sure how children recognize or decipher words. The mainstream of modern belief centers on children developing an almost automatic process of breaking words apart into the sounds that have been ascribed to those letters in words. They then reassemble the words and blend the sound representations into recognizable words.

At Neuro-Learning Systems we do not hold those beliefs. We feel that children develop an ability to store words and word meanings in their memory most likely by attaching sounds and meaning to the shapes that are represented in the formation of words. This would be just like the process they use in all visual recognition.

Syntactic Processing

Syntactic processing involves the ability to identify and use verb phrases, noun phrases, etc. Children are usually quite skillful in the use of these syntactic rules by the time that they enter school. This is a prime example of learning via modeling. Most, if not all children, can effectively use syntax but cannot identify it by name or structure. They have learned to use this process and are most likely unaware of it.

Semantic Processing

The development of semantic processing begins when children hear others use language, even before they can speak. The semantic process begins quite simply and expands as exposure to the outside world increases. The brain assembles meaning in logical networks. These networks start very simple and increase in complexity as the brain matures and the input of data increases.˜

These networks are semantic networks, or schemata. They contain more than just linguistic information. They mature to form skills, or networks of procedural knowledge. Semantic networks continue to develop throughout life as we perceive and experience new things.

Comprehension

Comprehension involves the use of all of the above processes. Comprehension is the ability to draw meaning from what we read and it is the reason we read. When children are new to reading and are reading in a hesitant manner, comprehension suffers. The speed at which a child reads becomes a critical factor in ensuring that children understand what they read.

Some children encounter obstacles in learning to read because they do not derive meaning from the material that they read. In the later grades, higher order comprehension skills become paramount for learning. Reading Comprehension places significant demands on language comprehension and general verbal abilities.

The National Institutes of Health has identified the following possible components of problems in comprehension: Inadequate background knowledge about the domains represented in the text; Inadequate understanding of the words used in the text; A lack of knowledge about different writing conventions that are used to achieve different purposes via text; Verbal reasoning ability which enables the reader to "read between the lines"; The ability to remember information; and The ability to read fluently enough without pausing to be able to keep track of the information presented. Almost all of the children we have worked with had a problem with number six only. Once this was "fixed" the comprehension problem was solved.

GETTING STARTED

Before you start, remember the power of your attitude. "Our lives are not determined by what happens to us, but how we react to what happens; not by what life brings to us, but by the attitude we bring to life. A positive attitude causes a chain reaction of positive thoughts, events, and outcomes. It is a catalyst...a spark that creates extraordinary results."

So that you may see extraordinary results, let's get started. The first thing you need to do is determine what level your child is currently reading on successfully. You cannot take anyone's opinion on this. Even if someone else has tested your child, you must make the determination. The only exception to this rule would be if someone with a Ph.D., who has no connection to your child's school, actually did the testing. Unfortunately, schools sometimes inflate test scores so that parents at least think their child is learning. This is not an official policy; individuals within the system do this. Most often, the test examiner is the same person responsible for teaching the student. The teacher helps the student with the test sometimes not even being aware that they are doing this. In over two hundred and fifty cases that we have tested, two hundred and forty four were not accurate. One hundred percent of the inaccuracies were inflated and none were deflated.

The other problem with testing is that most often teachers and others in the school system receive little if any training in test administration. If they get any training at all, they might get a couple of hours of lecture. This is not enough training. If it is true that you need more than a couple hours of training why would we suggest that you, someone that most likely has zero training, administer the test. The answer is simple; the test that we are asking you to give is designed with that in mind. If it errs, it will err on the side of prudence. You are the one most interested in this system working, you would not hamper that by "cheating" on the test.

Since it is always better to start easier than harder, the tests take this into account and starts you where you should start. To test your child, use the tests in Appendix A. Which test do you give? If you have an idea at what level your child is reading on, like second grade, start there. From there, move forward or backward to determine where your child fits. If you don't have a clue, start one level below your child's actual grade placement. Each test lists what is considered passing and what is considered failing.

These are informal tests and they should be used for what they are intended to be used, finding a starting point. They are not designed and they should not be used to determine anything else. If they err at all they will err on the low side. Continue to give the tests until you determine the highest level of test that your child can pass. It is important to start your child in the right place. Follow the directions given in Appendix A.

The higher level tests are tests comprised of lists of words. They don't really test reading or comprehension. Again, they simply give us a starting point. If your child can read at grade level or above but just does not seem to comprehend, they most likely have a fluency problem that is addressed in this book under "Advanced Readers."

After you have determined where to start, you will need to order books. The Houghton Mifflin Company publishes the books that we recommend. In grades kindergarten through third grade they are printed in black and white with no color pictures. We like these books for many reasons. First they are well thought out and contain the "high frequency" words that are so important to beginning readers. Second, printing them in black and white not only reduces the cost but it also reduces the amount of distractions that color pictures can cause. Next, the authors have done a superior job in determining the grade level of these books. This is no small effort and critically important. Many children's books are silly and boring. Although these are not exciting examples of literature, we have had very few complaints from students or parents.

You can find the list of books by grade level in Appendix B. We recommend that you order enough books to get you at least to the next grade level. For example, if your child will begin this program at the 2.1 level then you should order the books for 2.1 and 2.2; the next level is 3.1. Be aware of where you are in the list of books because it takes a while to get the books delivered. Make sure you order far enough in advance.

Do not supplement these books with books from school or your local library. The grade level of books is determined by many different methods. Asking your child to read a book that is too advanced puts him or her in the same situation that we believe got them in trouble in the first place. If you must read other books, be at your child's side and immediately tell them any words they don't know.

Attitude

Few things can be said with certainty when dealing with human beings. Attitude is one of those topics that we can discuss with a degree of certainty. In regards to this program, attitude is king. Everyone involved from student to parent to teacher *must* have a positive and pleasant attitude. We are 100 percent certain, based on brain research, that attitude can overcome grave disabilities. It can almost kill Herculean efforts as well. Show any sign of disappointment, failure, or other negativity and you are sure to be throwing your money (and maybe your last chance) away.

There is only one acceptable way to approach this task. We must all approach it as a serious job that will succeed! What does this mean? It means that the adults involved with this program must show, 100 percent of the time, the attitude, willingness, work ethic, and determination to succeed. Children count on the adults in their lives to "key them in" on what is good, proper, worthwhile, etc. They have built in "bull" detectors and they will see right through a phony smile. It is the job of the adults to insure that kids maintain a proper attitude. Just maintain this attitude: "We are on our way, I can see and feel success, we just have a little way to go." If you cannot truly believe this, you will be a burden to your child.

Now we need to look at the specific "things" to do or not do concerning attitude. First and

50

foremost, you must never, ever display any negative attitudes with your student. We would strongly suggest that you begin by telling your student that this is a new method of teaching reading and that it is much easier than anything they have ever tried. Tell them that they will not have to "sound out" words. (After they are good readers they will, but we suggest that you leave that part out.)

As a parent you have the greatest influence in the world, you can use it negatively or positively. Throughout this program, you should never be negative with your student. Never! If they have a bad day (or you do) and things are not going well, we suggest you say something like, "Let's stop for now, you're doing so great, I'm proud of you." Change the subject and look forward to a better start tomorrow. Be very generous with praise. After just one or two lessons, we think you will see enough improvement to make the praise sincere.

You should expect and be able to see success from this program. The success should be rapid. Please be cautious; many parents see rapid success and then expect too much or they do the opposite and slack off on the work. If it took your child six years of schooling to get in the predicament he or she is in, it will take nine to twelve months for them to reverse this process. Oddly enough, it seems that it takes most students nine to twelve months to become good readers. Most students will make rapid advancements and even move up one grade level every six to eight weeks. The typical student will need a good nine months of instruction to be fully ready to exit the program. Don't stop simply because they are now on grade level.

Attitude also relates to "homework." Don't skip it, ever. There will be emergencies and illnesses when it will be impossible. As soon as you stop for any other reason, you will gradually skip more and more. Before you realize it, you will not be doing the work at all. It is only fifteen to thirty minutes a day, what could be more important?

Whenever you feel that you are slipping, think of the pain that got you here. No one wants to endure that. Keep working and keep smiling. This isn't just good common sense, research supports it. Emotions color perceptions. Learning in a situation where positive attitudes are apparent help the brain to develop more and stronger neural pathways. Negative attitudes can actually prevent learning and memory from working. Negative attitudes cause the brain to produce a chemical that actually interferes with learning.

Planning for School

If your child is currently in school, you may have some major obstacles to overcome. You are going to be implementing a plan that is very different from the way schools operate. You can do this without their cooperation but you can make much greater strides with their help. This will probably not be easy. We have worked with dozens and dozens of schools, and only two, one in Kansas and one in South Africa have been easy to work with. In both of these schools, the students have made truly remarkable progress. The reason is obvious. Unfortunately, schools are not accustomed to working with "outsiders" directing the program.

Most schools will review our requests and program and tell you that this cannot work. Period. They tend to forget that if *their* program actually worked you would not be talking to them in the first place. They will compare our program to something they once read about or heard about but none will have actually used our program. This program began with us in 1998 as a research project. It was not made public until 2000.

You really will not want much from the school. You just want them to stop asking your child to guess at words they do not know. They call it "using context clues." We call that guessing. You also want them to not ask your child to do something impossible, read a book on the fourth grade level when their ability is at the second grade level. (Unfortunately you will find that in most schools 4th grade teachers only have 4th grade level books, 6th grade teachers only have 6th grade level books, etc.) There are other things you could ask for but you'll be lucky to get this. Read the story of Mark in the Kansas school in the case studies section to see what a school CAN do if they want to.

Unfortunately, we spend a fair amount of time testifying in court or at hearings to overcome these school situations. If your child has been determined to be "special ed," you will have another set of problems to deal with. Read the first case study for help in that area.

Schools are not places full of mean people. Schools are full of people and people generally have a great deal of problems with change. Many teachers that we have met also appear to have problems whenever anyone "intrudes" on their classroom. Most people outside of education do not realize that teachers are pretty much on their own when it comes to how they teach. They are "observed" by their principal as infrequently as once a year, with advance notice of that observation. (Really good school systems observe teachers six or seven times a year. Six or seven hours, out of 1150 teaching hours.) There is no good reason why any teacher should feel threatened and not welcome these adjustments for the betterment of a student.

Neuro-Learning Systems will send a letter to your teacher and principal if you think that would help. There is a nominal $5.00 fee for this service. You can write to us at: 25725 Long Corner Road, Gaithersburg, Md. 20882 or e-mail us at neuro@read.net. If you are planning to contact your school, please read the first case study before you do. It will show you what is possible when everyone works together.

Your First Lesson

Now that you have determined the starting point, it is time for your first lesson. Make sure your attitude is what we discussed earlier. Also make sure that you have read and understand this entire book, there are items presented later that may change the way you teach lesson one.

Take the first book in the series that you have determined to use. The list is in Appendix B. Sit down with your student at a table. A kitchen-type table and chair are best. Do not use a soft chair or sofa. Have your student sit so that their backbone is as straight as reasonable and at the same time comfortable. Make sure that the area is well lit. Natural lighting is best but not always available. Have your child drink a small glass of juice or eat some sugary treat. This is done because the brain uses sugar (glucose) when learning. (It should be obvious that you would not do this if your child is diabetic or has some other medical condition.)

Optimal room temperature is 67 degrees because the brain operates best at this temperature. If you can control the temperature, certainly you should. If that makes you feel a tad cold, wear a sweater. Your student can wear a sweater also but not a hat. A hat keeps the head warm and since that is where the brain is, it would be silly to make the room cooler and then wear a hat.

Begin the first lesson by explaining to your student that the brain can learn to read if only their eyes, ears, and finger all focus on the same thing. Tell them that while you are reading or while they are reading, you want them to follow along with their finger. They are to listen to your voice, follow the words with their finger and eyes at the same time. In the beginning, it may be helpful if you sit across from them and follow the words (from the top) with your finger as they learn how to follow with theirs. It really is not that difficult for you to read upside down but if you can't, just sit beside them.

As you read, move your finger under (or over if you are across from them) the word you are reading. It is important to read at a normal pace. It takes a little getting accustomed to but you and your child will learn quickly. Do not read more slowly than normal and make sure you don't "robot read."

Robot read means reading very choppy - one - word - at - a - time. You will have to be on guard not to do this and later to not let your child do this. You will be surprised how easy it is to get them to stop doing this. Just tell them and model for them the difference between reading choppy or fluently.

So, begin reading, read the first page aloud while your child follows with his or her finger. Stop at the end of the first page and have your child read the same page. They should use their finger as they read also. As they read, do not let them make an error. If they do not know a word, tell them the word right away. If they mis-state a word, give them the correct word right away. Have them re-read any sentence where they misstated words, NOT the sentences where they did not know and did not guess. Do not allow them to read incorrectly at this point. Correct all mistakes, even minor ones. You are finished the first page when your child has read the entire page without error. This does not mean that they need to read the entire page from beginning to end without error. It means that each sentence must be read correctly. In the beginning this may take awhile. At first, just make sure that they read every sentence correctly even if it means one sentence at a time.

Do the same for page two. Page two usually goes better than page one. The more you read the better they will become. Continue on for the rest of the pages in the book. At the end, your child will most likely be happy. Regardless of what happens, act excited and tell them how well they did. Hug and kiss and don't worry. Within a week, you will see things really begin to click. Most likely, you saw things today. Do not worry about phonics or comprehension, we will get to that later. You are done with lesson one of book number one of the level you started with. Yeah!

Note: The above lesson is for non-readers through third grade readers. If your student is reading above third grade level look at the section after this one that is titled "Advanced Readers."

There are important things you need to look for and be aware of for all lessons. We cover these under "Important Lesson Notes" at the end of the paragraphs on lessons. Make sure you read all of that before you actually begin.

Your Second Lesson

Lesson number two begins with the same book that you used in lesson one. Lesson number two is very much like lesson one. There is really only one difference, if this (reading one page at a time) appears easy for your child, you should group some pages together. Instead of reading one page at a time, read pages one and two and then let your child read pages one and two, and so on. This is a judgement call and it is an important call. You want your child to be comfortable but not bored. If you read pages one and two and your child has difficulty, go back to one page at a time. If they find two pages at a time easy, go to three at a time and so forth until you complete the book.

Lesson Three

Lesson three pretty much follows the same pattern as lesson two. If you can, go to reading more pages without interruption. You can even read up to half a book at a time if your child can keep up. Keep up means that they can read after you read with few mistakes. If you have to stay at one or two pages at a time that is okay but by lesson three your child should at least be reading two pages at a clip. If they are not, you should increase the "homework" or consider lowering the reading level.

Lesson Four

At lesson four you will model less and listen more. In lesson one through three you always read first followed by your child repeating what you read. In this lesson, read just the first page, then ask your child to start reading the first page and then continue on until they have finished the book. Today you will only model the first page. If your child is able to read the entire book with few mistakes, you should then discuss what was read. Ask who are the characters, what is the setting, and ask your child to re-tell the story to you in their own words. Ask a couple of specific questions such as, who did what, when? If there is any problem understanding this, have them go back to the page that answers the question and re-read it.

Please note that it is very difficult to read and comprehend a book when you are chopping it up the way we are suggesting. Don't worry, the comprehension will come later.

Lesson Five

This lesson will seem strange. For one thing we are going to read backwards....that's right, backward. If I read the first sentence in this paragraph backwards, it will look like this: strange seem will lesson the. Why? We want children to be able to identify these words as individual words, not as a page or group of sentences. After reading this book so many times, it would be simple to now "read" the sentences without even looking at the book. Students can learn a book the way they learn a song. That is not really a useful skill and that is not our purpose. When they read backwards, you will be able to tell immediately if they have learned to identify the individual words as we hope. Surprisingly, most if not all, kids love to do this. If they are unable to read these words backwards, it will tell you something critical, it will tell you that they are not focusing on the words with their eyes and finger. They are relying solely on their memory. You cannot let that happen. Insist that they focus.

Begin lesson five by asking your child to read the entire book (forward), hopefully without much help. At this point, if they do not know a word, give it to them but wait at least a few seconds to give them time to "find" it. As they read, encourage them to read as they speak, not pausing between words and with expression. As you get into later lessons you will want them to try to read at the speed they normally talk. After they read, do not forget to make a big deal out of it. Watch them smile about reading!

Next, ask them to turn to the last page and read the last page or two backwards. This usually sounds funny; if it does, laugh and let your child laugh. Laughter is a magical thing. In life in general, but even more so in regards to learning. We will bet that the funnier it sounds, and the more they laugh, the more they will remember.

Lesson Six

Lesson six is another critical point. You will have to make a decision based on how your child did in the first five lessons. Most children move well through the first five lessons. Occasionally, we encounter a child who has difficulty getting the "hang" of how this works. If your child has any difficulty moving through the first five lessons, repeat the first five using the next book on the list. If necessary, you can repeat the first five lessons up to four times. That would take 20 days, we have never had a child who did not get the hang of it before then. Only three percent of our students have needed more than 10 lessons. As we stated earlier, most of you will go on to lesson six and not repeat the first five.

If this appeared too easy you will have to make another decision. We want this to be easy, we want the child to succeed every time, every day. If on the first or second day your child is flying, maybe you should consider moving up a "reading level." A reading level is different from a grade level. Grade levels are K, 1, 2, 3, 4, 5 etc. Reading levels are usually referred to as R, PP1, PP2, PP3, 1.1, 1.2, 1.3, 1.4, 1.5, 2.1, 2.2, 3.1, 3.2, 4.1, 4.2, etc. Some tests report reading levels as 2.1, 2.2, 2.3, 2.4, 2.5 through 2.9 for each grade. They interpret this as 2.4 equals second year, fourth month. Reading levels are not an exact science and there are many methods to figure them.

If you are moving on to lesson six, continue reading. If you are returning to the first five, it would probably be best to stop here until your student is ready to go to lesson six. If your child did okay with the first five, go on to lesson six below.

Lesson Six begins a new book, use the next one on the list. Begin the sixth lesson just like the first lesson. Read the first page out loud while your child follows with his or her finger. Stop at the end of the first page and have your child read it. They should use their finger as they read also. As they read, do not let them make an error. If they do not know a word, tell them right away. If they misstate a word, give them the correct word right away. Have them re-read any sentence that they misstated words in, NOT sentences where they did not know and did not guess. Do not allow them to read incorrectly at this point. You are finished the first page when your child has read the entire page without error.

Do the same for page two. Continue on to the rest of the pages in the book. You read while your child follows with their eyes and finger. Then, they read, still using their finger. They re-read any sentence they make mistakes on until they have read every sentence correctly. Again, immediately give them any word they do not know. Do this until you come to the end of the book. You are done with the reading part of lesson six but now need to look at the spelling words.

The lists of spelling words are used for more than spelling. They also teach a little phonics and structural analysis but do not tell your student this. Start with the "an" words unless your child is all ready reading above the second grade level. If they are all ready reading at or above the second grade level, begin with spelling word list number 10 instead of number 1. You can find these lists of spelling words in Appendix C.

To present the spelling sections of this lesson write "an" on a piece of paper and ask your child what the word is. If they do not know, tell them. Ask them what "an" (say "an" the word, not "A" "N") becomes if they put a C in front of it? Say, "you know 'C' makes the 'Ka' sound in this word." Say, "So what is 'Ka' plus 'an' "? Tell them can if they do not know. Do the same thing for all of the words on the list. Then go back and ask them how to spell each word. If they get all of them correct, move to the next list tomorrow. If they miss any, make a note and go over the ones they missed tomorrow. Try to use the word in a sentence that has relevance to your child. The sentence; "Mary picked up the can." Mary being your child's name, is much better than "I see a can."

The spelling part of the lesson is independent of the reading. No certain set of words go with a certain book. Move through the spelling word lists as your student can handle them. Move to the next one when he or she can spell most of the words correctly. You have to use some judgement here. If he or she keeps missing one or two words, move on.

Also, make sure that you point out any small words that are found in larger words. For example: cat in scat, old and cold in scold. The more of these you can find the better for your student. Point them out and sometimes ask your student if they see any. We will present more on phonics later.

Lesson Seven

Lesson seven is identical to lesson two with a spelling component added. In lesson two you began with the same book that you used in lesson one. In lesson seven, you use the same book that you used in lesson six. Instead of reading one page at a time, read pages one and two and then let your child read pages one and two, and so on. This is a judgment call and it is an important call. You want your child to be comfortable but not bored. If you read pages one and two and your child has difficulty, go back to one page at a time. If they find two pages at a time easy, go to three at a time and so forth until you complete the book. Do the spelling lesson. This might be day two of the same spelling list or day one of a new list.

Lesson Eight

Lesson eight is identical to lesson three with a spelling component added. In lesson three you began with the same book that you used in lesson one. In lesson eight, you use the same book that you used in lesson six and seven. Unless your child is whizzing through these books, you use one book a week. Read two, three, or four pages then let your child read them. If you read pages one and two and your child has difficulty, go back to one page at a time. If they find two pages at a time easy, go to three at a time and so forth until you complete the book. Do the spelling lesson next in order.

The spelling lessons are actually spelling, phonics, and structural analysis lessons rolled into one. <u>Do not</u> refer to them as phonics lessons. Many children totally turn off when they hear the word phonics. Phonics turns them off because they have not been successful with phonics. We advise that you not use that word until they are much better readers. "Sound it out" is the same as saying phonics.

Lesson Nine

Lesson nine is just like lesson four with a spelling component added. At lesson nine, you will be modeling less and listening more. In lesson one through three and six through eight you always read first followed by your child repeating what you read. In this lesson, read just the first page, then ask your child to start reading the first page and continue on until they have finished the book. Today you will only model the first page.

If they are able to read the entire book with few mistakes, you should then discuss what they read. Ask, who are the characters, what is the setting, and ask your child to re-tell the story to you in their own words. Ask a couple of specific questions such as, who did what, when? If your child has any problem understanding this, go back to the page that answers the question and re-read it.

If they are not able to read it with few mistakes, skip the final part above. Instead have them read the book again.

Lesson Ten

As you may have guessed, lesson ten is very similar to lesson five. In lesson ten we want the student to read the entire book (forward), hopefully without much help. At this point, if they do not know a word, give it to them but wait at least a few seconds to give them time to "find" it. As they read, encourage then to read like they speak, not pausing between words and with expression. As you get into later lessons you want them to try to read at the same speed that they normally talk. It is critical for your child to learn to read at least at the speed that they normally talk. Comprehension, we believe, is strongly tied to reading speed. Check it out yourself. Read something very slow and you will find that your mind wonders and does not remember what you read. After they read do not forget to make a big deal out of it. Watch them smile about reading!

Next, ask them to turn to the last page and read two to four pages backward. As we said earlier, this usually sounds funny, if it does, laugh and let your child laugh. Laughter is a magical! You will not be asking your child to read parts of the book backwards every fifth lesson. You might just ask them to read a couple of pages backwards at the conclusion, or fifth lesson, of each book.

The Next Lessons

As you have probably noticed, there is a pattern forming here. The reading lessons are in groups of fives. Most parents teach these Monday through Friday and then use Saturday and Sunday to just read or do homework. Spelling lessons are pretty much free form so that they follow the individual learner. Each set of lessons begin a new book. Do not skip anything. You will probably become bored with the book after five days but remember that repetition is a big part of this program. We have had only one or two problems due to the repetition. With the right attitude on the adult's part, this works fine. It is imperative to follow the order of the books that can be found in Appendix B. There is only one exception to this rule, if your child can read the entire book without missing more than two words (proper nouns don't count) go on to the next book.

From this point forward, you should conduct the lesson as discussed below.

1st Lesson – Parent reads a page or two at a time, students reads after parent. Spelling lesson.

2nd Lesson – Parent reads one, two or three pages at a time, student reads same amount. Spelling lesson.

3rd Lesson – Parent reads either one, two, three, or more pages and the student reads the same amount. Spelling lesson.

4th Lesson – Parent reads only the first page. Then student reads the first page followed by all the other pages without the parent reading them first. If they are able to read the entire book with few mistakes, you should then discuss what they read. Ask, who are the characters, what is the setting, and ask your child to re-tell the story to you in their own words. Ask a couple of specific questions such as, who did what, when?

If your child has any problem understanding this, go back to the page that answers the question and re-read it. If they are not able to read it with few mistakes, skip the final part above.

5th Lesson - Begin by asking your child to read the entire book. At this point, if they do not know a word, give it to them but wait at least a few seconds to give them time to "find" it. As they are thinking of the word, make the beginning sound of the word. For example; if the word is "shape," make the "sh" sound. We will want them to do this in latter lessons. You are now beginning to model this. As they read, encourage then to read as they speak, not pausing between words and with expression. Do not forget to get them to pause at the end of sentences. As you get into later lessons you want them to try to read at the speed they normally talk.

Every other week, you should ask them to read two to four pages backward. This will tell you if they are learning to recognize words or not. After they read, do not forget to make a big deal out of it. Watch them smile about reading again!

This is the core of this system. Does it seem easy to you? It should because it is easy. We have successfully trained many individuals who have no teaching background. In fact, we have trained many teachers to use this method and most were not successful! It certainly appears to us that a background in teaching makes using this system more difficult. We think we know why. Teaching in schools is a very difficult job when done correctly. This method is easy. Teachers either fiddle with it or they think that they can make it even better by doing this method and then adding this or that.

If you are not a teacher, just follow the above guidelines. If you are a teacher, believe us when we say, "Do not add or delete ANYTHING!" Anything means just that. We have had many teachers say that they are following our program and then we observe them and find out that they are not. They have made what they feel are minor adjustments. We do not see it that way.

A typical example is as follows. Many, if not most, teachers have been taught that one of the first things they should do in reading class is to ask the students to look at the book-cover art work and make a prediction about what the story might be about. Many teachers write down these predictions and then go back to them at the end of the lesson to see who was correct. They call this predicting we call this "guessing" and think that this is the root of many students' problems. We would never do this and we totally disagree with the school of thinking that suggests this. This kind of exercise is why students insert words that do not belong because they have already decided what the sentence is about. What could they gain from this? (Teachers should also read "A Special Note to Teachers.")

Important Lesson Information

Is this all there is to this system? No, but it is the main part. Remember we said that Neuro-Reading was "A.R.M." attitude, repetition, and modeling. Can you see where each fit in? If you do this and nothing else you will be very successful but there is more that will advance students even further.

In Appendix A, you will find a set of tests to give your student. The main test was to help you find a reading starting point. The other tests and checklists were to determine where there are "holes" in your child's education. These are important as well as necessary in helping your child move to a higher level of reading. After your child has advanced through 20 lessons or so, it is time to begin adding these "missing parts."

Find the phonics checklist and make a list of the phonic sounds that your child missed. Do not work with a copy of the test, it is a little intimidating for kids if they recognize it. Just make a list, short o, long e, j, u, etc. You then need to find words that have these sounds. Be sure about the words you choose, if in doubt, leave it out. Do this in advance of the lesson. Vowels are hardest but most important. Alternate; do a consonant first, then a vowel, etc. until you go through the complete list.

Try to cover phonic sounds that match the spelling words you work with. For example, work on the short "a" sound when you are working on the "an" family of words. This coordination is not mandatory but it is the intelligent way to go.

Choose one a week. Start on your second lesson of the week. After the reading lesson do this phonic lesson in place of the spelling lesson. Ask your child if they know what sound a _____ makes. If they know, ask them to think of a word where this would be found. If they know that, you are finished. If not, tell them what sound it makes and then show them three or four words that have that example. Show and say the words and sounds and have them repeat after you. It is important for them to see and say them.

Repeat this lesson on your fourth lesson of the week. Again, let it replace the spelling lesson. This should only take a few minutes. On your fifth lesson have a brief review of the phonic lesson and a brief review of any spelling words you have worked with. DO NOT make a big deal of these phonic lessons! Many students become agitated just when they here the word phonics or "sound it out." Cover the material in a matter of fact manner. You must be careful, this can undo what you have accomplished if you put much emphasis on it.

After twenty or so lessons, you should also look for opportunities to informally teach "structural analysis". This is not as complicated as it sounds. Typical structural analysis is expanded somewhat here to include not just prefixes, suffixes, root words, and compound words but also to include any "small word" that may help in identifying an unknown word. Again as with the phonics this should not be emphasized a great deal.

Simply pick a word or two from your book that has a small word in it, such as "candy." Candy has a "can" in it or "biggest" has "big" in it. We simply want you to point these types of words out once or twice every lesson after you have done the first twenty lessons. Later we will do more with this on a more formal basis.

There are a number of words that give students a difficult time. Most of these words can be found below. If there is a dash – between two or more words it indicates that these words are sometimes confused with each other. These words are, we believe, one of the foundations of reading problems. They tend to frustrate everyone. You need to be aware of them and tell them to your student as soon as they pause, <u>before</u> they have time to form more improper neural networks. We have found that most students take a very long time to be able to read these words correctly. You have to help them build the correct neural pathway to these words. If the word naturally falls at the beginning of a sentence, students are even more lost. Tell them right away and prepare yourself to tell them many many times. The only way they will "get" it is to read them thousands of times, and they must read them correctly. Don't ever say, "I just told you that word." If they could read it, they would.

It is interesting to note (and probably a key to understanding the problem) that all of these words are words that you cannot form a mental picture of. Words like wagon or dog are not on the list. Another note about these words, be happy if your child does not ask you the meaning of the word "the" or "was." Could you answer that question? These words share something else in common, they are some of the most commonly used words in all of writing. They have been our students biggest problems.

Most Confused Words

This
These- those
Them – then
Was – saw
Of – off – from – for

What - that
Where - which
There – their – they're
Stay – way – may – any short word with "ay"
Every – even – ever – very - other - over
Her – she
Come – came
Once – one – only – other – another
Now - know
When – then
It – is

You need to be aware of the words that throw your student for a loop. Don't write them down in front of your child, but do write them down later. Take five of these words and five other words that they DO know. Type a list in 12 point font or higher. We want you to do something with this list.

Everyday after you have this list we want you to begin your lesson with it. Put the list in front of your student, tell them that these are words they might need to work on. They are to put their finger under the first word as you say the word. After you say it, they are to say the same word. They move their finger down to the next word, you say it, they repeat what you say. They MUST look at the word as they say it! Continue down the list. After the first time, at your next lesson, tell your student that you are going to try to do this fast. DO the same thing but try to do it very fast. Make sure that you and they are saying the word AND that they are looking at the word as you say it. This can really help even though many people believe that reading words in isolation is a different skill than reading. Continue to read this list but don't always start with the same word. Sometimes start at the bottom of the list, sometimes in the middle and so forth. After awhile, re-type the list in a different order.

About every fifth day test your student. Ask them to read the list without you reading it first. If they pass, save the list and re-check them every once in awhile. Make another list of words that they are having problems with and begin anew. We believe that this process takes advantage of a little know process called priming.

Movement

The first thing that we look for when a student is having problems is their level of movement. It is not necessary to remain perfectly still while reading but we believe it is impossible to read unless the student sits relatively still. We have had many students with severe A.D.H.D. who were very able to maintain the amount of stillness necessary. The eyes must have a chance to focus on the word to be able to read it (at least for a milli-second.) It takes less than a tenth of a second for the eyes to view and the brain to process a word. We have found that, when asked, A.D.H.D. students have plenty of control over their movement. We simply explain the importance of sitting relatively still.

While speaking of movement it is important to understand another kind of movement, how the eyes move while someone is reading. The eyes do not sweep across the page and then return to the other side like a carriage return on a typewriter. It is normal for eyes to move in quick back and forth jerky fashion.

As long ago as 1879, reading researchers noticed that the eyes move in jerky motions. At the University of Paris, Professor Javal called these, left to right and right to left, quick jerks "saccades", the French word for "jerks." The eye is looking ahead and behind during these jerks. The brain is looking at new words and rechecking words just read. Although you are not aware, your brain is actually processing words ahead of you while you are reading. If you closely watch someone read you clearly see these movements. Many people think that there is something wrong when they are not familiar with this process.

Advanced Lessons for Low Level Readers

This section is for students who have started at the low end of the reading ability scale and have advanced a grade level or two. The section for those currently reading at the 4.1 reading level and above is later in this chapter.

What we include here is for a student who meets the following criteria:

Began below the 3.1 reading level.
Has advanced at least one full *grade level* with this system, i.e.: went from 1.1 to 2.1 in *reading* level.
Show signs of at least the beginnings of confidence about reading.
Sometimes self-corrects while reading.
Is not having an attitude problem.

For those that meet the above criteria, we want to begin to add a few details to their instruction. We have found that a child can advance from a non-reader to grade level 3.1 without any additional training other than the "adult read, student reads" method. To advance beyond the 3.1 reading level and to become accomplished readers our studies indicate that a student needs to learn other things not yet formally addressed. No one will be able to figure out every unknown word that they will encounter unless they know some phonics. As reading levels increase so do the complexity of words…that is actually what determines if a composition is to be designated a 3.1 or 4.2 reading level.

In our "Introduction to Phonics" we want you to begin very simply with modeling. When a child pauses at a word they do not know, we want you to tell them the word but we want you to emphasize the beginning sound of that word. For example, if the word is snake, you would say, "Sssssss nake", if the word is "butter" you would say, " B b b butter. Do not ask your child to do this at this point, only you do it. Do this for two to three weeks. Do not say "Bah" for B, just make the sound of air coming out of your mouth with a beginning "B" sound.

After you have modeled the beginning sound for many words you will begin to ask your student to shape his lips/mouth like the beginning sound of words they don't know. With most students, this is magical. If they form their mouth correctly, the word comes out. As incredible as this seems, it happens 75 percent or more of the time. Do not ask them to guess! We never ask them to guess. Just say this, "When you come to a word that you don't know, look at the first letter. Shape your lips like the sound that the first letter makes. After you do that, look at the whole word and see if you know it. You will not believe how successful students can be using this simple method.

If they shape their mouth incorrectly, show them how. When they are shaping their lips, you should be doing the same so that they can see you. If they say the incorrect word, correct them right away. If they say a word that does not even start with the same sound, explain how this cannot be correct. You will want them to do this from now on. Tell them that once they shape their lips this way, if they do not know the word they are to look in the word for smaller words.

You should have been modeling this search for small words from the beginning. You should continue to model this until they are proficient at it. You should tell them words that they do not know and that have no small words in them. We do not want even the slightest amount of frustration in regards to figuring out word pronunciation.

Once your student has become proficient at looking for small words and shaping their mouth like the first letter sound you will be ready to begin to teach them how to sound out words.

Another issue for readers beginning either the 4.1 level or sometimes the 3.2 level is the huge transition that is often a stumbling block. Going from 3.2 to 4.1 often means going from books with many pictures to books with no pictures. It often means going from pages with ten or so sentences to pages with fifty or so sentences. It usually means going from larger print to smaller print and from few multi-syllabic words to many of these words. This transition can really throw kids for a loop. We have found it to be helpful to make a copy of the fourth grade text, and either cut it up in to smaller "pages" or better, re-type it and change the font to a bigger font. We put fewer words on a page and try to make it look like the lower level pages. We have the student read this and then we show them the original page. We explain how they were successful with the more difficult material and explain how some students let themselves be intimidated when they first see the higher level material. This has worked in the vast majority of cases, sometimes the student will need to be reminded of this later.

Phonics

This is the only section of the book that I was not thrilled to write. It is within this section that I am sure to make some enemies. That is clearly not my intent but it is clearly what will happen. I should begin by stating that I believe that every child should learn phonics. I also want to tell you that I became a very strong reader without mastering phonics. I also need to tell you that ninety-three percent of the people who have taken an elementary phonics test on our web site, and identified themselves as elementary school teachers, failed the test. You can take the test at: http://www.neuro.read.net/Form3.html if you like. What does this mean? To me it can only mean that phonic skills are not as important as the entire world of education tells me they are. I am not exaggerating when I say the entire world of education. All of the "research" points in that direction, all except a few others and ours! I have to say that all of the research that I have reviewed has one thing in common, they never ask people to read in their testing. They ask them to perform some type of non-reading task and then make the huge assumption that the non-reading task says something about reading.

I have read numerous books that promote phonics with almost a religious fervor. One well-known book states that it is impossible to learn more than 1000 to 1500 words as sight words. The same book notes that you need to learn 44 phonic sounds and then be able to blend them effortlessly in tens of thousands of combinations. That just is not true. Many if not most of our clients have attempted to mediate their reading problem by purchasing a well-known phonics game or a phonics program. Whether they actually used the game or not is unknown but they then came to us because their child still could not read. One well-known researcher "proves" that phonics is the key by taking images of the brain of good readers and poor readers. She then declares that the pictures of the brains are different and it is because one knows phonics and one does not. Couldn't it just as easily be that one brain is reading using some yet unknown process and the person who has that brain just happens to know phonics also? Or that the person who knows phonics learned phonics NOT by being taught phonics but by learning to read another way and extrapolating the phonics. Or any of another hundred possibilities? The brain sees what it expects to see; "we" need new eyes.

Having said that and NOT saying that we are positive of everything, we think it is advisable to introduce our students to phonics. We do this after they have reached a third grade reading ability level. We do not place a great deal of emphasis on this because we are certain that the teaching of phonics to our students has been a painful experience. We have been very successful, we feel, because we have not taught this as a do or die scenario.

We have advised you to introduce this in your reading lessons via modeling. We also asked that you briefly touch on this as you do the spelling words and as you do mini-phonic lessons. When you are at a stage to teach this level, we refer you to Appendix C. In Appendix C you will find a phonics inventory. Complete the phonics inventory so that you do not waste time teaching skills that have already been learned. Determine which phonic skills your child is missing. Introduce these skills as outlined below. Remember, be positive, be specific and probably most important, be brief.

Based on the information you glean from the phonics inventory you should have a list of the beginning phonic sounds that your child needs to remember. Do not be surprised if your child already knows all of the sounds. Do not worry if they know few. Simply take your list and pick the first one. The best way to introduce and teach these sounds is by modeling. Find the sound in the book that you are working with. Point it out as you or your child are reading it. Throughout the week simply point out and state the sound that the letter represents. Do this two to six times the first day, two to four times the second day and two or three times the third day. On the fourth and fifth days, ask your child to point it out to you two or three times.

Do not make the mistakes that many teachers make. Many teachers do two things that confuse children. First, they pronounce the phonic sounds incorrectly! Second, they confuse the letter name and the letter sound. Both of these are extremely confusing. Many teachers make the same pronunciation mistake on many letters. To make the sound louder they add a short "a" or "ah" sound to most letters. They say, What letter makes the "Cah" sound? The sound that comes out of their mouth sounds like "Kah". "C" does not make that sound. "C" makes the sound of air coming out of your mouth as if starting with a "K" sound. If children think that "C" equals "Kuh" than cat would be pronounced "Kuh-at." The other mistake they make is inter-changeably using the letter name and the letter sound. You cannot do this. The system is confusing enough, make sure that you refer to what you intend to refer to.

Comprehension

One of the first things that teachers ask, after they ask about phonics, is about comprehension. How do we handle comprehension? When we began this program, we had no new way of teaching comprehension. We were using the old method of asking children to visualize what they were reading, etc. We also coached students in how to visualize.

We never went beyond this because we never had to. Every, let us repeat that, every student we ever taught had near perfect comprehension at the end of our reading instruction. We went back and looked at this. We found that children entering the program had poor comprehension. Children in the middle of the program had poor comprehension. The same students near the end of the program had almost perfect comprehension. Even students who "had memory problems" had good comprehension.

We believe that comprehension is a function of reading fluency. At the end of our program when reading speed is emphasized, comprehension goes up dramatically. We realize that this may not be true for every child but it has certainly been true for the hundreds of students that we have seen. If you read slowly, you will find that you become lost very quickly. Even if you are able to keep up you will find that you will get bored quickly. Both of these are the death of comprehension.

We have never really had to teach comprehension per se to our students. Every one of them have learned comprehension with almost no effort that we could observe. They were able to do this by simply being asked to read smoothly and having someone model what they were doing (reading in a choppy manner) and then model what they should have been doing.

Since this book was first published we have had a number of students enter our program that could read just about any word, yet had little comprehension. We have been highly successful with them but simply teaching them to read smoothly and at the rate that they speak. The vast majority of these students read choppy and/or slow. We simply model the correct smoothness and have them re-read that same passage trying to read smoothly. We also model the correct speed as well as putting feeling in their voice. The trick to reading speed is to read the same speed that a child speaks to a parent or brother/sister. Many of our students have been in college and for the most part their problem was reading too fast. They were in a hurry to get through the material and they lost comprehension in the process.

Although most needed weeks of practice, all were able to increase their comprehension dramatically. Students who were able to improve their "reading with feeling" were the ones who made the largest gains in comprehension. All students were successful in using this method.

Homework

Homework depends on your particular situation. Is your child in school? Is this summer break? Do they have lots of other homework? The perfect situation for a parent would be to begin the program a week after school ends for the summer. If it is September now, do not use that as an excuse, time is of the essence. Start now and make adaptations as described below.

If you are beginning this program in the summer time or if you are a teacher using this at school, handle the work in the following way. Do the lessons in the morning and do the homework described below in the late afternoon or early evening.

If you are starting this program during the school year, do one of the following schedules. Do the lesson before school and do the homework in the early evening. If that is not possible, do the lesson as soon as you can after school and then do about half of the homework later that evening or the next morning. If you work and cannot get to these lessons until six p.m. or so, skip the homework all together.

Homework is important. If the material is presented and reviewed later the brain will retain much more material, much quicker. That is the purpose of homework. If you can do it at all, do it. If other homework gets in the way, worry about the lessons first. We hope that you can take advantage of the days you do not work. On those days hopefully you can do a lesson early and homework later. We strongly recommend that you do these lessons six days a week. Seven days is okay too. If you must, five is okay. If you cannot do this five days a week, you are wasting your time. We have found in our research that this requires a minimum of five days. We have found that six days of lessons and six days of homework are optimal.

Many of our parents have conducted this program as follows. On the two days that they do not work, they teach a lesson in the morning and do homework at night. On three of their working days, they do a lesson as early as they can. On the remaining two days they do just the homework on one day and nothing the other day. We also know of parents that teach these lessons at home in the morning and take their child to school a little late each day. You would need to coordinate this with the school in advance.

We are reluctant to say this but many people have been successful with two lessons a week and six evenings of homework. This is how Neuro-Learning Systems has conducted its telephone tutoring service. The major difference is that we are expert at teaching these lessons. Again, we suggest that you follow one of the examples above.

As for the actual homework, it is very simple. Your child reads the same book that you are using in the lesson. He or she uses his or her finger. You do not read first. You sit next to them and immediately give them any word that they do not know. Try to anticipate words they don't know and say them before the child has a chance to say them incorrectly. When there are spelling words that go with a lesson, you go over them and talk about them. (We explain this further in the lesson section.)

Advanced Readers

For the purpose of this book, advanced readers are those students who are reading at or above the 4.1 reading level. For these readers we have to make certain adjustments. Before you decide to use the advanced approach, make sure that your student is reading at or above the 4.1 level (not counting comprehension). We have tested many children who had been told they were at or above this level when they were clearly not. It is highly critical to begin at a level where your child is. As stated many times in this book, do not trust the school system to supply you with this information. They are too involved to be objective and we have found that they rarely are accurate.

We have used this system with people reading at the twelfth grade level and they were able to advance their abilities. This system does have limits. It cannot take a child who is eight years old, in third grade, reading on a third grade level, and advance them to fifth grade reading ability. It appears that this system can only erase problems, it cannot create gifted readers. If you are an adult reading at a fourth grade level, you should be able to use this system to bring your reading level up to 12th or college level. (You can not do it by yourself, you will need an accomplished reader to help.)

If your child is reading on a 4.1 through ninth grade level, you should do the following. Those reading above the ninth grade level should begin with the second part of this section. If they are reading at the 4.1 or above level we have to make certain assumptions, the first being that they know phonics and can "sound out" words. If they do not you should take the phonics inventory provided in the testing appendix and start from there. If figuring out words is no problem for them follow the program described in the next paragraph unless they have a comprehension problem.

If they have a comprehension problem but are able to make it through most reading material on their grade level you have a special circumstance. As discussed elsewhere in this book, we believe that comprehension problems are reading fluency problems. Increase fluency and you increase comprehension. Finding your starting point is complicated. You want to start at the level where the student has good fluency. If they are 18 and cannot read first grade material in the same manner and speed in which they speak, you will have to start at first grade level. After you find the level, follow the remainder of guidelines in this book. Remember the key is to be able to read quickly, the same speed as you informally speak. You help a student do this by modeling what they are doing, reading choppy, and then model what they should be doing, reading smoothly.

The student should follow all the guidelines mentioned earlier. To recap: sit straight at a desk or table, in a cool room, with good natural lighting, elevate blood glucose by drinking a small glass of juice, the student must use his or her finger to guide them when they or their teacher is reading.

Start the reading program with material on their level, not above their level. The teacher reads one page and then the student reads the same page. Do this until it appears easy. Then the teacher will read three or four pages followed by the student reading the same pages. Do this until it appears easy. Advance like this until the teacher is reading an entire chapter followed by the student reading the same amount. The lesson should last as long as the student is comfortable, up to forty-five minutes.

During the next lessons, you will most likely be comfortable starting at the five to six page level or maybe even the chapter level. During the even numbered lessons you should read five or six pages using the Neurological Impress Method. We usually start the lesson with the typical process, teacher reads, and student reads. Then we do five or six pages of the Neurological Impress Method. We follow this with more of what we started with until our time is up.

The Neurological Impress Method is described below. The Neurological Impress Method was developed after WWII to teach brain-injuried soldiers to read again after having suffered a severe brain injury. It has been used successfully with those who have had strokes and with others recovering from traumatic damage to the brain. Though it has never entered the mainstream of teaching techniques in public schools, it is sometimes used by "special education" teachers working one-on-one with students.

One good point about this procedure is its ease of use. Most people can easily learn the steps needed to implement the Neurological Impress Method.

To follow the NIM method of reading instruction, the steps are:

1. Determine the student's instructional reading level, this is very important.
2. Prepare to work with the student for five to six pages.
3. Sit side by side in a manner comfortable for the student. The way you both sit is very important.
4. Determine which hand the child uses to write and eat with. If it is the right hand, sit on that side. If it is the left hand, sit on that side.
5. Place your body slightly back from his/hers, so that your mouth is in line with his/her ear. Do this so that the student cannot watch your lips and hears your words directly in his/her ear.
6. Jointly hold the book you are reading between you.
7. You hold one lower corner and she/he holds the other lower corner with his/her non-writing and non-eating hand.
8. Take his/her writing hand in yours and have him/her form a fist with the index finger extended. Place your hand around his/hers so that you can guide his/her index finger to keep it below the word you are saying. (After your student becomes proficient at following with his

finger, you can let them do it without your hand.

9. Read orally together the words keeping your voice about one and one-half beats ahead of his/hers. This allows him/her to do the following:
   A. Hear the word just before she/he says it.
   B. Correct any miscued word before she/he finishes saying it.
   C. Intone the language correctly by imitation.
10. Stop every few paragraphs and ask comprehension questions to be sure the student understands the text being read. The more interaction about the text the better.

Parents'Frequently Asked Questions

1. Will my child learn phonics with this approach? Yes, but not in the usual way. Although there is direct instruction in phonics, most of our phonic instruction comes via modeling.
2. Why these books? We selected the books very carefully for two reasons, first, they exactly represent certain grade level abilities and second, they are rich with high frequency words. In the English language, 100 words make up 75% of all non-technical writing.
3. My child is memorizing these little books. Is that okay? Yes, we want them to BUT we want them to read them focusing their eyes on the words as they say them. That is why using the finger is so important. We want the brain to make a correct neural path for these words.
4. I heard that using the finger slows you down. We heard that also but it is ridiculous. Anyone

can move their finger 50 times faster than they can read or follow. It's just one of those crazy things that have been around so long that no one knows where it came from.

5. Is there a "key" to this system? Yes, it is sugar coated, highly emotional, repetition and modeling. Much the way you learned to speak (and taught your child to speak.) Do you remember repeating, modeling, and cheering the first "Mommy's"?

6. Is reading to my child important? Yes, very important, children cannot figure out a word unless they have heard it before. They might get close but they will not be sure unless they have heard it spoken. They also need to hear fluent reading, reading that flows smoothly. Hearing it from you is best. Reading to them is good modeling.

7. I am not a good reader, does number six above apply to me? Sorry to say but no it does not. If you have serious problems reading it is better if you do not read to your child.

8. Why didn't the schools teach my child this way? Two reasons, no one knew of this method until recently and schools are set up to teach 30 students at a time. This method does not work with 30 students at a time.

9. What should we do when these lessons are over? Please do not ever stop reading 15 minutes every night with your child until they are reading at least on a 6th grade level preferably through high school.

A SPECIAL NOTE TO TEACHERS

If you are a college trained teacher this chapter will be of special interest to you. First, we want to tell you what our experience and research tells us. Unfortunately, teachers have the toughest time with this method of teaching reading. They have problems because it is very different from what they have become accustomed. Additionally, when attempting to apply these principles, teachers tend to either add things or they make other adjustments based on their training. Both practices destroy this program!

When we first used this method commercially, certified teachers were hired to implement it. In short order the certified teachers were replaced with people who knew nothing about education. These tutors did fine. The problem was that teachers added, subtracted, or otherwise altered these methods. When they did that, they met with huge failure. The failures became apparent quickly. They could not make the adjustment. Even when loss of employment was evident, teachers could not make the adjustment.

Of course, we do not see this as an impossible task but we do see this as a tough task. Our advice to you is simple to state but difficult to implement. If you use this program, make zero alterations. If it is not in this book, don't do it, say it, or even think it.

A good example is how many teachers ask students to look at the book cover and make guesses about the subject of the book. This is not only a common practice but it is also one that most educators accept as a good thing to do. We strongly believe that this is a negative practice and would never suggest that a child do this. We want children to *know*, not guess. We think you should leave predicting to the fortunetellers. As you can see in our method description, guessing about the story or about individual words is NOT allowed.

There are many other "things" about our program that go against conventional thought. We believe that is one of the reasons we are so successful. Teachers are trained in conventional thought. If you cannot put that training aside, you will not be successful with this program. That is not a small task. Teachers must stay on guard at all times to prevent backsliding.

Another issue of interest to teachers is similar to what was just discussed. Another trap which teachers fall into is this; once they get this program going "as is", they tend to try to embellish the program thinking that this will only make for larger success. It just does not work. Follow this program to the letter, make zero adjustments and be thrilled with the results. If things are not going well, first look for the minor adjustments you made out of habit, even teeny tiny ones.

The above is not an indictment of teachers or schools. It is simply a statement about what works with this method and what does not work with this method. If what you do is successful then, by all means, continue to do it. You do not need this book. If on the other hand, you do need this book, give it an honest try. It is not like professional development programs you have attended where you take what you want and leave the rest. This is a complete package. We have experimented with many combinations of these methods and others. What remains is what works as a unit. It should also be noted that what we have developed for schools is slightly different from what we have developed for individuals. We all know that teaching twenty-five students at a time is far different than teaching one. Approximately fifty percent of what we do at school is identical to what we suggest that people do one on one. The other fifty- percent could be used at home but it involves equipment and preparation that is not usually found in the home.

In preparation for publication, many teachers read this book. Some came away feeling that there were indictments against teachers in this book. We hope you do not feel that way. We are not trying to indict anyone. We do feel, however, that there is a lot of room for change in schools. Change is difficult for everyone and we understand that. We also understand that a lot of water goes under the bridge (with children drowning in it) while teacher's feeling are being protected. Frankly, we think that the adults and their feelings need to take a backseat to student success. We know and if you are a teacher, you know also, that a lot of things go on in schools that shouldn't.

We also want you to know that we were successful with this program with children who, sadly for them, had parents that did not care. Also with parents that were drug addicts and parents who were illiterate. We successfully worked with children whose parents were mentally retarded. We found out that we could make the difference in these kids' lives with or without the parent's help.

We also found out that even the worst parent wants their child to be able to read.

Many teachers feel that derelict parents are a cause of student poor performance and see that as a reason for their failure. We see derelict parents as a reason to try harder and make a difference in the child's life. It is a tough world out there and if you are a child and have derelict parents, you are pretty much doomed. If you add the inability to read, you are almost assured of a career of crime and poverty. If you teach that same child to read, statistics show that you have reduced the chance of him or her going to jail by at least fifty percent.

Take our reading system, find the doomed child, teach them to read and you will know the feeling of walking on air. We bet you will rediscover the reason why you first wanted to teach. Do the impossible once and you are hooked, you will do it again. It also has a magical way of making all the little annoyances we find in school feel much smaller.

Classroom Adaptations

If you plan to use this in your classroom, you will need to make very few adjustments. This program is used very successfully in large and small classrooms. We have used it in classrooms with the very traditional three reading groups. Each group usually has six to nine members. As with most educational endeavors, the smaller the group the better. We have had very successful groups of ten. As with traditional groups, reading levels should be as close as possible. Unlike "newer thinking" regarding groups, round robin reading is a hallmark of this program. Not the traditional round robin where children figure out what part is theirs and only read that part. This round robin requires that everyone participate at all times. While one child reads the other children follow with their finger. The teacher reads first as in the "home" version of this method. The only real modification to the home version is that you have to let six or so children take turns reading instead of one child reading everything.

Some aspects of the larger groups actually make this program a little easier. When other group members are reading everyone else must follow with their finger. Aha, you say, they'll just go through the motions. Not so! They will be turned on to the fact that they are doing so well and because you are lavishing them with well deserved praise. We have had the worst behavior problems disappear in this program. Everyone intrinsically knows the tremendous value of reading. The speed and ease of this program can reach even the unreachable.

In addition to the "home" version there are other things that you can do in the classroom that are difficult to do at home. The outline is below. We suggest that they become part of your reading time but they could be used at any time. We will present them as we recommend they be done. The group lesson can be adjusted somewhat as to time, grouping, or frequency.

Either using an opaque projector (which would be best) or an overhead projector, project a page of reading material on a screen or wall. The material should be whatever level you teach. If you teach third grade and you have readers from 2.1 through 4.1, use 3.1 reading material. Use _.1 material where the _ is the grade you teach. Although this material may be above or below some students' abilities, this will be educational regardless. Attempt to make the projected words as large as possible. Research suggests that the size of the letters is important. They must appear (as a projected image) to be at least 2 inches tall. Then simply read the story to the children while you follow with your finger or a pointer. Obviously, students need to focus on what is going on. Read the story at least twice, three times is better (not on the same day). That is it!

Students are exposed to print and the words that the print represents. Not only do children benefit as they would in any read aloud, they also benefit much more from viewing the words as they are said. There are programs currently being taught where this is the only enhancement to traditional reading methods. While results are preliminary, they are remarkably promising. In one classroom where this was tested, every child in the room was reading at or above grade level after just twelve weeks. Only 44 percent were on grade level prior to the program.

The other classroom adaptation involves the use of a tape recorder. We recommend that you use this procedure as part of the rotation of reading groups. Using material appropriate for the groups' instructional level, the teacher must record a book on an audiotape. This should not be the same book that you use in the reading group. Students (as many as you have headphones for) listen to a tape of the teacher (or adult volunteer) read the book while they follow with their finger. They do this every day until they have mastered the book and can read it without error. We recommend that who ever makes the recording include brief reminders to turn the page and use your finger. When the student is able to read the entire book with very few errors, give them free reading time until all group members finish. Once all group members finish, a new tape (book) is used. In the schools that tested this method, they made charts to keep track of the individual's progress. They also reported using aides, volunteers, and others, including the principal to listen to children read to pass them to the next book. This program has also produced remarkable results.

What about homework? Homework should be the same as the individual program. As for the actual homework, it is very simple. The student reads whatever book you are using in the lesson. He or she uses her finger. Parents do not read first. Parents sit next to them and immediately tell them any word that they do not know. The parents' main role is that of cheerleader.

We are reluctant to write this but we want you to understand this system completely. We have taught this system in public schools with children who came from dysfunctional families. Many of these children did not do the homework. They were still able to learn to read! They did not advance as rapidly as others who did the work but they did advance. We suggest that, if possible, you group these children together. That way they can move along but just at a slower pace. Another option is to group the students by reading level and as they advance, re-group them again according to reading levels. We also understand that these same children may need to be separated due to behavioral concerns.

If you are a special education or reading specialist teacher we want you to be aware of something. While it seems obvious that one on one instruction would work best, our research indicates that this is not the case. One on three, followed by one on four, followed by one on two, followed by one on one are actually the best situations. Current federal government research has come to the same conclusion. Why? We aren't sure but we think that it has to do with three things; one, children sometimes learn best from each other, two, they actually hear the words read more with more people and third, there is the desire to keep up with peers

Teachers' Frequently Asked Questions

1. Are you sure there is enough phonic instruction in this program? Yes, Read our research results. There's enough for major success.
2. Will this work in my classroom? Yes, we have taught this in public schools successfully.
3. Can I be trained in this method? Yes, contact our office. (We usually have a waiting list.)
4. You emphasize fast pace, why? When you are behind, you need to catch up and going slow bores kids to death. Comprehension is also lost.
5. Won't special education mediate reading problems? Most special education teachers do two things that kill a student's attitude. First they slow things down and then they only work on what the child CANNOT do. Who wants to

be in that environment? Both of these things foster horrible attitudes regardless if the child displays the feelings or not.

6. How can you get better if you do not work on the things you are weak on? You do work on these things but you also do the things you are successful with in order to maintain your positive feelings about learning. You start with what you can do and build.

7. Why haven't I heard of this before? Two reasons, it is just two years old and these principles of brain research were recently discovered in 1996 - 1999. A few in 2000.

8. I feel like you are saying that everything we do in school is wrong. No we are not. Schools are designed to teach many children at the same time. It works for only about 45% of kids. Schools do not address those above or below the average.

9. Is this like any other program? Yes, it takes pieces from many different programs. It derives most of its principles from current brain research. It is much like the process in which you learned to speak.

10. Isn't speaking innate? It was once thought to be but recent studies have proven otherwise. You may have heard of the study at U.C.L.A. with the 12 year old who had been abused by being kept in a room alone. No one spoke to Genie for ten years. This, as well as other studies have proven that speaking is a learned behavior.

CASE STUDIES

We present case studies here to give you an idea of how these principles can work and some of the complications you could encounter. The first case study demonstrates how a school can cooperate if they wish. Most of the schools we have worked with have been difficult to work with. Some have been literally impossible to work with. We have spent a considerable amount of time in court and at hearings advocating for our students.

Mark

Mark attends school at Jefferson Elementary School in Kansas. Mark's father has literally searched the globe trying to find a way to help his son. He and his wife have spent great amounts of time and money trying to figure out what was wrong. Mark's father found Neuro-Learning Systems on the internet.

Mark appeared to be an average eleven-year-old boy in the fifth grade. He likes all of the stuff that boys this age like. He is a handsome young man that has an older brother. The first thing you notice about him is how quick his mind is, quick to joke, to think, and to enjoy life. One would never guess that he had any problems.

Mark was having considerable problems in school. His school said he was reading on a first grade level and was just slightly higher in other areas. He was identified as a special education student and received a significant amount of support in the "resource room."

I met Mark in late June and tested him in reading. He scored as a non-reader or "readiness level" as many schools call it. He seemed very eager to learn and please. He also displayed many of the classic symptoms of Attention Deficit Hyperactivity Disorder. He seemed a little immature for his age but also seemed quite normal in all other aspects. His neurological tests were unremarkable. I noted how eager he was to please in regards to the reading tests. His tests were terrible! It was obvious that he was simply guessing at every word. I was not surprised how poor he did; I was surprised that he got anything correct. On the word "red" he might guess "ride" or "watch." There really was no rhyme or reason to his guessing. It was the worst case of guessing I have ever seen.

After testing, I talked to Mark about school. He started by telling me how much he liked school but only gave me terrible stories about school. He lowered his head and quietly told me that no one wanted to play with him at recess and that many boys he knew called him "retard." He told me that he liked science and math but that he could not read any of the science or math material. He said that Mrs. R, that's his nickname for her, and Patty were nice to him but that he wished he didn't have to visit them everyday in the resource room. He told me that children teased him about going there. He also told me that he had overheard a teacher say that he was retarded. I asked him if he thought he was and he very quietly and softly said, "No."

After I scored the tests, I told Mark that he was definitely not retarded. I told him that I thought he was actually very bright. You could see the relief on his face. I told him what I thought the problem was. I told him that I thought that when the school was trying to teach him reading in kindergarten, he was not ready. When he was ready they were far ahead of him and that he pretty much had taught himself a coping strategy....guessing.

I told him that I was sure I could teach him to read and all that he had to do was stop guessing. (No small task!)

I tutored him over the telephone twice a week for five months. That brings us to the present time. While I was eating dinner last week, Mark called me at home. He wanted to share that he had just taken a 5th grade math competency test and had passed all but one part. He also had just received his report card and was on the honor roll! He is currently reading like a champion on the 3.2 reading level with no end in site! He will most likely be reading on or very close to grade level before this school year ends.

His dad tells me that he has many friends this year and there is always someone visiting at the house. His Aunt Becky says that she thinks he even looks different. His mom and dad are so proud of him they cannot contain themselves. They love when Mark talks about going to college, etc. and I am sure he will.

There are four remarkable stories here. First the story of Mark. How can a kid be beat down for so long and so hard but never give up? Mark did it, he is an inspiration to all of us. The next remarkable story is of Mark's parents, just like Mark, they never gave up. Next is the remarkable story of how this reading system could not just help someone to read but have the ability to alter lives forever. The last remarkable story is about Mark's school. Jefferson Elementary came together as a school and said, "What do we need to do?" Mark's dad and I told them.

At a meeting during August when no one was supposed to be working, many people choose to come to school to form a plan. I flew from Washington, D.C. to Kansas. At the meeting were Mark's parents and Aunt Becky, the principal Mr. Atkinson, the special education teacher, the counselor, and Mark's two teachers for the coming year. Mark has two teachers because they are "job sharing," each teaching half a week.

After I told them what I felt Mark needed, Don Atkinson, the principal said, "I don't see why we can't do all of that." Everyone else agreed. I was amazed. This was at least the fiftieth meeting where I had made similar requests, this was the first time I had heard those words. Since then I have attended more than fifty more meetings and I have only heard those words once more, in South Africa.

What these people had agreed to was what I thought was the absolute best case scenario for Mark. They were going to do all of the following. His special education teacher was going to work strictly in the background. No one would be able to identify him as a special education student. No more visits to the resource room.

Mark would go to Mrs. Boger's second grade classroom during reading period in order to read second grade level books to the second graders. Mark and his classmates were informed that this was an honor position as assistant teacher. While he was there he would also listen in on the second grade lesson that was going on. After he "tutored" the second graders he would listen to a tape of me reading a book on his instructional level.

He would then return to class where his two teachers, Mrs. Debbie Koelsch and Mrs. Robin Niederee would make sure that he was successful. They would modify tests and materials to accommodate his lower reading level. And they would hold him accountable, just like everybody else, for his own behavior. Whenever humanly possible they would treat him like everyone else, which is what he wanted more than anything. They allowed Neuro-Learning Systems to direct his reading program. They also agreed to ask him to read aloud only if he wanted to and to not ask him to "predict" or guess at words.

This "experiment" worked for only one reason, this principal, and these teachers found room in their heart to help a child. It meant a lot more work for all of them. As time progressed and they could see and measure Mark's success, they became even better at what they were doing for Mark. They have literally changed the world, without them this child's future was bleak. Now, anything is possible. I am sure they do not realize how special they are. Mark's mom and dad know! Mark on the other hand just thinks he's one of the guys.

John

John's case is somewhat unusual in that he was part of our study group. We present his case here for a variety of reasons. By reading John's case we think you can see how strong this system is and how continual reading is important.

John was a third grader in Mrs. Cyndi Tremper's class. He had been a special education student since first grade. He liked math and could do math much better than other subjects. He was reading on a kindergarten level. He was a personable child who was verbal and quick to smile. He was lucky to be in Mrs. Tremper's class because she is a very lively and personable teacher who has more patience than most. Since she is also quick to smile, I thought they would be a perfect match.

John, like most kids, loved our reading program immediately. It was towards the end of the year when we began with John. He had already started hating school and was beginning to think that he would never learn to read. I spoke to his parents about this program and they were delighted to have John take part.

John picked up the program rather quickly. We took over his reading instruction; he received no other reading instruction other than what we gave him. We worked with him four days a week when he was in school. John was always late for school and absent just a little more than most children. We gave him homework every night and he did it only on rare occasions. When we talked to his parents about this, they said that they would take care of it. They took care of it by lying and saying he had done it when he clearly had not. John would even tell us that his parents had told him to lie about it.

John's teacher and parents noticed John's improvement right away. We had started John at the 1.1 level and he quickly moved through the entire first level series. Within one month, John was reading at the 2.1 level. At the end of the second month, school ended. At that point, John was reading at the 2.2 level. He had come a long way in a short time and his parents were ecstatic.

John was part of a group of five. All but one had started at the kindergarten level. All progressed at about the same rate. The ones that were doing the homework were noticeably stronger readers.

Since summer was beginning, we had a meeting with John's parents. We stressed to them the need for John to continue to read over the summer. We also told them that, at this stage in his reading development, they would have to be actively engaged in his reading. We also told them that we predicted that John would lose all that he had gained if he did not read almost every day. We gave them a detailed list of things to do and a list of books to use. We also gave them four books to get them started. They assured us that they would do this.

Since we had seen his parents fail to follow through continually, we called them twice during the summer. We reminded them of the need to read and they told us that John was reading every day. His dad said, "Yeah he's reading books and even signs we ride by in the car."

When school restarted we met with John and asked him to tell us some of the books he had read. He very flatly told us that he had read zero books. We encouraged him to tell us about one book he had read. He again stated that he had read nothing. We tested him and the school reading specialist tested him. To no one's surprise, John was back at the kindergarten level. His parents were actually mad as if someone else was to blame. His father told us that he felt that by now the school should have "fixed" John.

The other four students had slipped back either a very little or none at all. Two of the four were later dismissed from special education and are doing fine in reading and school in general. The other student moved and we were not able to contact them.

Tina

Tina is a twelve year old going on eighteen! She wants to be older and acts and looks that way. She was in the special education program at her middle school. She had been diagnosed with mild mental retardation. She had never learned to read but for some reason had still maintained an interest in reading and learning.

Her teacher, Ms. Gilla, asked if we could work with her. This was near the end of school and we did not want to take on any new students. We finally agreed to her teacher's constant begging. We were only able to see Tina twice a week. Her mother was excited and promised to work with her on the homework.

Tina was a success from the first day! See had never read even one page of a book before. She left the first day, reading a small 1.1 reading level book. She was so excited that she re-read the book to her teacher and the classroom aide twice after she returned to class. Her mother said that they read the book at home, then cried for an hour, read it again, and cried again.

Tina was the best student to work with that we have ever had. She would have stood on her head and read if we had asked her to. She stayed focused 100 percent of the time. She left every lesson excited with her new book and could not wait to read it again to someone, anyone. She completed the entire first grade reading level in five weeks.

The second grade level books were much harder on Tina and she began to lose confidence. We countered that with a conference of the adults. At the conference, we all agreed that this was a critical time for Tina and that she needed tons of encouragement. She got the support and the love she needed to see her through. She made it through the 2.1 and the 2.2 series in about six weeks.

Summer arrived and we taught Tina's mother how to work with her. We went back to school at the beginning of the year and tested Tina with the Woodcock Johnson test. Tina scored at the 4.6 level on that test. That equals approximately the beginning of the 4.2 reading level. We suggested that she be re-tested in all areas. The school said no but her mother insisted.

After testing, Tina moved to the regular education classes. Her tests showed "average intelligence." This is not supposed to happen but it did. Tina is probably the happiest girl in middle school. She is still behind but she is closing the gap. If we showed you a picture of Tina before and after you would never believe it was the same person.

Tina's mom thinks we know everything. She wants us to help get Tina's mind off boys. This program cannot do that.

A FINAL WORD

Almost everyone who has ever reviewed these lessons and almost everyone who has ever witnessed the lessons being given said the same thing, "This can't work!" We not only understand that but we were at least two years behind because we felt the same way. We saw it working, we tested to prove it was working and we still thought there was something else that we were not seeing. We understand how this is difficult to understand, especially if you are a teacher.

It is noteworthy that we have offered a money back guarantee when we professionally administer this program and that we have never been asked for even a penny back. We have even had grateful parents donate thousands of dollars to fund other children's programs.

In education and in life we all want simple solutions. We want everything to be short and easy and we are even willing to sacrifice quality somewhat. When we finally find something short and easy, especially when everything else we have looked at was difficult and long, we find it hard to believe. That's human nature and more than not that is a fact of life.

We really hope that you will not let that kind of thinking blind you. Like all good teachers, we are out to change the world with this book. Talk to any judge and they will tell you that prisons are overflowing and they are overflowing with people who cannot read. Reading is the critical life and education skill. We have also personally witnessed the "world changing" things this program can do.

When you see children fully bloom from the low point they once were, you will become a believer also.

We have to change the world one kid at a time. You might as well begin with your kid. Read every word in this book, then read the "Getting Started" at least twice. Follow every guideline, especially the ones about attitude. You will see a most remarkable transition. Not only will your child blossom but so will you, just by watching them and knowing that you were the one that made this happen. You were the one that found this program and you were the one that read it. There is nothing worse than being forced to stand-by while your child suffers. When you cannot or do not know how to help, the pain is much worse.

Now you know how to help! Do not let the mundane details of life prevent you from doing this everyday. Sure you have to work and eat and sleep. Sure work wears you down and you need a break. Put off the breaks and whatever for just a few months. You will never regret the effort or the time you spent with your child. You will never forgive yourself if you don't.

We have tested this program using parents as teachers. We did not want to write this book without knowing the ins and outs. We received several telephone calls from parents during the testing. They called because "things" were not going so well. In one case, there was an unusual circumstance; the remainder of the problems were caused by one of two things. Either attitudes needed adjustment or there was a commitment problem on the part of the adult. Adult commitment problems were the biggest problem. Treat these lessons as if you were administering critical medicine. If your child does not get it, they perish.

There are few sure things in life. We honestly believe that if you let this opportunity pass you by you will never forgive yourself later when your child's pain becomes much more severe. Children who cannot read have shorter life expectances, fewer employment opportunities, and and fifty times the normal risk of spending their life in jail. They are ten times more likely to abuse drugs.

Please, just do it. Later write us a letter and share your joy!

A closing thought. *"A hundred years from now it won't matter what my bank account was, the sort of house I lived in or the kind of car I drove...but the world may be different because I was important in the life of a child."*

Appendix – A

Tests and test information.

General Testing Information

This appendix contains tests for reading levels and inventories of phonic and other skills. You should probably start by testing your child for a starting reading level. Once that is completed, you will still need to administer the other inventories in order to assess what information is missing from your child's reading education. We recommend doing this over a number of days so that boredom or annoyance with the test will not be a factor.

There are two completely different types of tests for reading levels in this appendix. Reading levels 1.1 through 4.2 are listed first. They are traditional tests where a student reads a story. Tests to determine levels 5 through 11 are listed next. These tests are much simpler and involve reading a list of words only.

Do not confuse *reading level* and *grade level.* Schools most often speak of *grade level,* some tests such as the Woodcock Johnson give a score on *grade level.* We most often discuss *reading levels* in this book. Grade levels appear to be more precise but they are not. A child reported to be reading at the 2.3 *grade level* is most likely reading in a 2.1 *reading level* book, and so is a child on the 2.4 *grade level.* There are no such things as 2.3 grade level books. A child that is reported to be reading at the 2.7 grade level is most likely reading in a 2.2 reading level book. In essence the 2.1 reading level book covers 2.1 through 2.5 grade levels, the 2.2 reading level book covers 2.6 through 2.10 grade levels. The grade level stands for years and months thus, a 2.6 grade level is second grade sixth month.

If that is not confusing enough, there are three levels for each child. A child will have an independent level, an instructional level, and a frustration level. They are usually listed in this order. The independent level refers to the level of book that a child can read with no help and still understand what he is reading. The instructional level refers to the level that a child is currently working. If left to their own, the child would have some difficulty but should be able to understand a good deal of the material on that level. The frustration level is that level of books that a child would fail at, they would understand little, if any, of what they were reading. Typically, it would work like this for an average reader in third grade at the beginning of the year. Their independent level would most likely be 2.2, their instructional level 3.1 and their frustration level either 3.2 or 4.1 (All levels are reading levels not grade levels.)

For this program, you will most often use reading level. The tests in this appendix report a reading level to start on, based on a score. You will order books based on the reading level. You will only need to know grade level when talking to teachers and when reading school reports. If your child is in a special education program, you need to be aware of what level they report to you, reading level or grade level. You almost never need to use independent or frustration levels. Usually, schools speak in terms of instructional level. This program also speaks of instructional reading levels.

Giving the Tests

To give these tests you need to have a general idea of your child's reading level. If you do not, do not panic, there is a way around this. If you know or think you know their reading level, start at that level. If you think they are reading on the 2.2 level, give them the test for the 2.1/2.2 (Green) reading level. The tests cover a school year, 2.1 and 2.2 (Green) are the same test. The difference comes in the scoring. Similarly, the 5.1 and 5.2 are together.

If you do not know and cannot make an educated guess, you will have to start with their grade level. Not grade level reading ability, just grade level. If they are in third grade, give them the 3.1/3.2 test (Yellow). If they are in the third grade but you know they are reading way below, it would be best to give them the 2.1/2.2 test (Green).

Score the tests simply by counting the number of words the student does not know. If they get the entire test correct, give them the next hardest one. If they get the entire test wrong, give them the next easiest test. Continue to do this until you give a test that the child scores at a particular level. You will begin with this reading level. You will order the same level of books. This is not an accurate measure of what level your child is actually on.

Take the score your child receives and begin at that level. Order books at that level and the next level. If your child scores at the 2.1 reading level you will begin this program at the 2.1 reading level and you will need to order books at the 2.1 and 2.2 reading level. If they score at the 2.2 reading level, you will begin this program at the 2.2 level and order books at the 2.2 level and 3.1 level. Levels above third grade are not divided like 3.1 3.2. They are fourth, fifth, 6th, etc All children except advanced users begin at the beginning of the spelling program. /

We designed the tests to give you a starting point – nothing else. It would be unwise to share these scores with your child's teacher or anyone else. They do not apply to anything other than this program.

To give the test simply let your child read the page. The first four are color coded so that they do not tell your child what level they are. The color code is below. When they read the test do not tell them any words or help them in any way. Tell them to skip the words they do not know. Keep a mental note of how many words they miss. Ask them to read the title and the paragraph when giving either test one through four.

Tests fifth through eleventh grade are different from the first through fourth. They are word lists and you are to score them a little different. On the word lists, the student reads the list. Take note of words they miss. The reading level is the list of words that they read and miss only two words. If they miss more than two words, give them the next lowest list. If they miss, one or no words give them the next higher list. These tests do not look at comprehension.

Color Code --- Blue = First, Green = Second
Yellow = Third,   Red = Fourth

Test for Grade Level - Blue

House in the Woods

Would you like to live in a house in the woods? I went to visit a friend who lives in a house in the woods.

When I walked in his house, it was noon. Even in the middle of the day, it is a little dark in the house. That is because the trees in the woods block the sun.

If you live there, you can see many animals. There are also many places that you can hide if you are playing hide and seek.

At night, I think it would be a little scary. It would be too dark.

Scoring the First Level Test

Scoring the test is simple. Simply count the number of words missed. If a student misses the same word twice, it counts as missing two words. There are 113 words including the title.

If they miss five or more words, you should start them in this program with the 1.1 series of books. If they missed two, three, or four words, you should start them at the 1.3 level. If they missed zero or one word you should give them the Second Level Test. If they get five or more wrong on that test, start them at the 1.4 level.

Remember, this test is for this program only. It does not imply what level your child is on, you need a more comprehensive test than this one to tell you that.

Test for Grade Level – Green

The Race

Every year our school has a race in the spring. This year my best friend Steven entered the race. I went to the race to cheer Steven on.

Steven loves to run. He runs just for fun with his father. Steven and I though that he would win this year for sure. Steven was the oldest student in the race since he is in fifth grade. In this race, every one runs together.

When the race started, Steven moved out in front. Nobody was even close. He continued to lead the race until the final quarter mile. At that time, someone pulled up close to him. It was his sister Patty! Patty was a great runner but she was only in third grade. Steven thought he had to win. He could not let a third grader win.

Patty and Steven were side by side. The crowd was going crazy. At the last minute they held hands and timed their pace so that they would finish at the same time

Scoring the Second Level Test

Scoring the test is simple. Simply count the number of words missed. If a student misses the same word twice, it counts as missing two words. There are 170 words including the title.

If they miss five or more words, you should give them the first level test. If they missed two, three, or four words, you should start them at the 2.1 level. If they missed one or zero words you should give them the Third Level Test. If they get five or more wrong on that test, start them at the 2.2 level.

Remember, this test is for this program only. It does not imply what level your child is on, you need a more comprehensive test than this one to tell you that.

Test for Grade Level – Yellow
Our Trip

Last week we flew to the Bahamas. We went there to visit our family. We have not seen them in a long time. As our airplane approached the islands, we could see the clear blue water below. It was so very pretty. When we got off the plane, we could feel the warm air gently surrounding us.

Our family greeted us and welcomed us to the beautiful island. They explained to us all the wonderful things to do while we were there. They invited us to have dinner at their house in the evening. Then they dropped us off at our hotel.

We checked in at the hotel. We ran to change our clothes and splash in the beautiful water. We spent most of our time at the beach frolicking in the water. We were unhappy to know that it was time to depart. When our plane lifted off, we could see the beautiful water again. We will never forget the beautiful water. Someday, we hope to return to the Bahamas.

Scoring the Third Level Test

Scoring the test is simple. Simply count the number of words missed. If a student misses the same word twice, it counts as missing two words. There are 172 words including the title.

If they miss four, five, or more words you should give them the second level test. If they missed two, or three words, you should start them at the 3.1 level. If they missed zero or one word you should give them the Fourth Level Test. If they get five or more wrong on that test, start them at the 3.2 level.

Remember that this test is for this program only. It does not imply what level your child is on, you need a more comprehensive test than this one to tell you that.

Test for Grade Level – Red
I Love the Circus

I love the circus. Even when I was a child, I enjoyed going to the circus. I especially like to observe the silly clowns. I laugh and laugh at their ridiculous antics.

I also take delight in the circus animals. I like to watch as the people ride atop the elephants and watch the trainers as they perform with the lions and tigers and bears. I frequently wonder why these strong animals don't attack their trainers. I'm pretty sure that I would be too frightened to attempt to perform with them.

I also relish the food at the circus. I realize that it probably is not the best food for you but I still enjoy it. I especially enjoy the polish sausage. Sometimes my stomach becomes upset when I eat them but that's okay.

I even considered joining the circus once. That idea didn't last too long though. I realized that it would not all be fun and games. Plus, I would not get to see my friends except when the circus arrived in their town.

Scoring the Fourth Level Test

Scoring the test is simple. Simply count the number of words missed. If a student misses the same word twice, it counts as missing two words. There are 177 words including the title.

If they miss four, five, or more words you should give them the third level test. If they missed two, or three words, you should start them at the 4.1 level. If they missed zero words, you should give them the Fifth Level Test.

Remember that this test is for this program only. It does not imply what level your child is on, you need a more comprehensive test than this one to tell you that. These tests do not look at comprehension either.

It should be obvious that the following tests are for a general idea NOT to determine someone's reading level. They do NOT look at comprehension at all.

Test for 5th Grade Level

scanty
business
amazed
considered
discussed
behaved
splendid
acquainted
escaped
grim

Test for 6th Grade Level

bridge
commercial
abolish
trucker
apparatus
elementary
comment
necessity
gallery
relativity

Test for 7th Grade Level

amber
dominion
sundry
capillary
impetuous
blight
wrest
enumerate
daunted
condescend

Test for 8th Grade Level

capacious
limitation
pretext
intrigue
delusion
immaculate
ascent
acrid
binocular
embankment

Test for 9th Grade Level

conscientious
isolation
molecule
ritual
momentous
vulnerable
kinship
conservation
jaunty
inventive

Test for 10th Grade Level

zany
jerkin
nausea
gratuitous
linear
inept
legality
aspen
amnesty
barometer

Test for 11 th Grade Level

galore
rotunda
capitalism
prevaricate
risible
exonerate
superannuate
luxuriate
piebald
crunch

Appendix – B

Books and Ordering Information.

Books

At the lower grade levels we use books that are published by the Houghtin-Mifflin Company. We use these simply because they are the only books that we have found that are very accurate in reading level and printed in black and white. We want them black and white because we feel that this cuts down on the distractions that color pictures cause. If we could figure out a way to do it, we would use books with no pictures at all. We do not want students guessing based on the pictures. This is the way they are taught at school but we think that is a major mistake. The books are printed on "news print" paper so they are not as expensive as they could be. These books contain all the "high frequency" words that we want students to read and their sequence is perfect.

Unfortunately, the books only come packed in school set-ups. They are packed by grade in multiples of six. The 1.1 through 1.5 are a package, the 2.1 and 2.2 are packed together as well as the 3.1 through 3.2. This is only a problem if your child falls in the middle of a grade level. For example, if you need to start at the 2.2 level, you have to buy the 2.1 and 2.2 books together. So to be ready you would have to buy the 2.1/2.2 package and the 3.1/3.2 package.

You can order books from the Houghtin-Mifflin Company directly but you will have to buy six of each or the color books. We think the color books are a big mistake. The color books distract the reader and take their focus away. This is very important in the early years. Although we do not want to become book sellers, we are willing to buy these books and resale them to you as individual units as opposed to the six at a time the publisher requires.

Once you get beyond the 3.2 level you will be ordering books more like what you are used to. We recommend that you order the entire series that we list below. When ordering these books, you will be ordering individual books. Some of these books are also available at most large bookstores on the internet and in your communities. Many are at public libraries. The 1.1 through 3.2 black and white books are not. We will also sell these books to you.

If you would like to purchase the books from us, please turn to Appendix D. We have listed the procedure there.

First Level

1.1 Wake Up
The Hen Sat
Snuffy, Fluffy and the Mice
Jump, Jill, Jump
Me Too!
Ian and the Seed

1.2 Our Plants
A Walk in the City
A Fish Trip
Where is My Baby
Fox and Chick
Hank and Lin

Second Level

At the fourth grade level the books that are available are more traditional "chapter books." These books are treated just like the smaller books except you have to make a determination as to how much you will read as homework and how much you will read ahead aloud before your student reads. Many times you can use a chapter as if it was a mini book. If you are starting at or have advanced to the fourth grade level, make sure you read the section on "Advanced Users".

The following books are the ones we recommend. They are part of the Invitations to Literacy program at Houghtin-Mifflin Company. You can order the books in Appendix D. (In grades 4 through 6, Houghtin-Mifflin also has a large hardbound book that has numerous stories in it. They are anthologies and are listed in case you prefer these to the individual books.)

4.1 Anthology = Imagine
   Freckle Juice
   A River Ran Wild
   Cam Jansen and the Mystery at the Monkey House
   Radio Man/Don Radio
   Uncle Jed's Barber Shop

4.2 Yang the Youngest and His Terrible Ear
   Misty of Chincoteague
   The Mystery of the Hidden Painting
   Justin and the Best Biscut in the World
   Stone Fox
   The Enormous Egg

5.1 Anthology = Explore
The Mouse and the Motorcycle
Come Back, Salmon
The Hundred Penny Box
Head for the Hills
Skylark
The Kid in the Red Jacket

5.2 From the Mixed-up Files of Mrs. Basil E.
Frankweiler
Rascal
Dear Mr. Henshaw
Volcano
Old Yeller
The Whipping Boy

6.1 Anthology = Quest
Long Claws
Strider
Zekmet the Stone Carver
A Young Painter
Mop, Moondance, and the Nagasaki Knights
Sharks

6.2 Hatchet
A Jar of Dreams
Pompeii: Nightmare at Midday
Tuck Everlasting
Number the Stars
Deep Sea Explorer

7 Roll of Thunder
Sweetgrass
The Root Celler
Waiting for the Rain

Izzy, Willy-Nilly
A Long Way from Home
A Swiftly Tilting Planet
Beowulf, A New Telling
The Hobbit
True Confessions of Charlotte Doyle
Woodsong
Children of the River
Black Star, Bright Dawn
Across the Great River

8   The Westing Game
Willie Bea and the Time the Martians Landed
Child of the Owl
Let the Circle Be Unbroken
The Contender
April Morning
Summer of My German Soldier
The Voyage of the Frog
Invitation to the Game
Citizen of the Galaxy
Homecoming
The Pigman
The Legend of Tarik
Dragon of the Lost Sea

Books Above the Ninth Grade Level

We have not listed books above the ninth grade level for an important reason. A student at this level is going to be negatively affected seriously if you ask them to read a book that they do not like. Attitude at this level is even more important than at the lower grades. Interests can be wide and varied.

Students at this level need books that they are interested in and that they have the ability to read. We strongly recommend that you choose books with your student in conjunction with a good librarian. If your student finds that difficult, we recommend that you ask them for subjects they are interested in and then visit the school or local community librarian. Stress to the librarian that you want books on _____ grade level that are about the subject _____.

Books at this level are not as specifically graded as they are at the lower level. Most books at this level will report a grade range like eight through eleventh as opposed to a single level. At this level reading is much more about experience with reading than it is about specific words or skills.

Appendix – C

Spelling and Phonic Lesson
Materials

1. The an family

ban
can
man
pan
ran
van
fan
plan
than
span

2. The it family

bit
fit
hit
sit
kit
lit
skit
spit
slit
split

3. The ot family

got
hot
lot
not
pot
rot
plot
shot
spot
trot

4. The ing family

bing
king
ping
ring
sing
wing
bring
sting
swing
thing

5. The in family

bin
fin
kin
tin
win
chin
grin
skin
spin
thin

6. The ill family

bill
fill
hill
pill
mill
ill
will
spill
still
grill

7. The ut family

but
cut
nut
rut
gut
hut
jut
shut
strut

8. The ug family

bug
dug
hug
jug
mug
rug
tug
drug
plug
snug

9. The ock family

dock
lock
rock
sock
block
clock
flock
shock
smock
stock

10. The og family

dog
bog
fog
hog
jog
log
clog
frog
smog

11. The un family

bun
fun
run
sun
spun
stun
bunny
funny
runny
sunny

12. The en family

den
hen
men
pen
ten
tent
then
bend
when
mental

13. The ell family

bell
cell
fell
sell
tell
well
yell
shell
smell
spell

14. The est family

best
nest
pest
rest
test
vest
west
chest
guest

15. The et family

bet
get
jet
let
met
pet
set
wet
net
yet

16. The ay family

day
hay
may
pay
ray
say
way
clay
stay
play

17. The at family

bat
cat
fat
hat
mat
rat
sat
pat
flat
that

18. The ack family

rack
black
tack
back
track
smack
pack
snack
sack
jack

19. The ail family

jail
hail
mail
pail
sail
tail
fail
nail
rail
trail

20. The ain family

grain
rain
brain
drain
chain
pain
train
plain
gain
explain

21. The ake family

snake
rake
lake
make
take
bake
shake
stake
flake
sake

22. The ame family

flame
frame
lame
blame
name
fame
game
shame
came
tame

23. The ank family

bank
rank
tank
blank
spank
sank
plank
yank
clank
flank

24. The ap family

cap
gap
sap
nap
lap
slap
flap
trap
clap
wrap

25. The ash family

ash
smash
crash
trash
flash
cash
thrash
mash
bashful

26. The ate family

ate
mate
hate
date
late
gate
plate
slate
state
skate

27. The aw family

paw
jaw
law
saw
claw
straw
draw
lawn
hawk
brawl

28. The ea family

eat
eagle
meat
bean
treat
lean
cream
stream
jeans
sneak

29. The ight family

might
night
fight
right
tight
light
sight
slight
height
flight

30. The ick family

chick
pick
stick
sick
trick
brick
kick
pickle
bicker
cricket

31. The ink family

ink
drink
think
blink
wink
stink
shrink
slinky
wrinkles
tinker

32. The oa family

boast
coast
roast
float
coat
gloat
goat
moat

33. The ade family

bade
fade
jade
made
wade
blade
grade
shade
spade
trade

34. The aid family

laid
maid
paid
raid
braid
staid

35. The ance family

dance
lance
chance
France
glance
prance
stance
trance

36. The ool family

cool
fool
pool
tool
drool
school
spool
stool

37. The oon family

coon
loon
moon
noon
soon
croon
spoon
swoon

38. The ore family

more
pore
sore
tore
wore
chore
score
shore
store
swore

Basic Phonic Inventory

Show your student the page that follows this explanation. Ask him or her to tell you the sound that each particular letter represents. As you know, some letters represent two or three sounds. A sample of the sound for each letter appears on page 2. If your child gives you one sound for a letter that has two sounds, ask them if the letter stands for any other sound. Keep a brief note of the letters/sounds missed.

You will use this inventory in determining the phonic lessons that you will need to offer your student. Many people have found it easiest to copy both pages. They show their child page one and make an underline on any sounds missed on page two. It is important that the student not see your "key" page or the marks you make. This brief inventory should give you an idea of what to teach your child later when instructed to do so.

Page 1 of Phonics Inventory

b	c	d
f	g	h
j	k	l
m	n	p
r	s	t
v	w	x
y	z	a
e	i	o
	u	

b boy   c cat city   d dog

f fat   g got gentle h hop

j job   k kite   l lap

m mom   n nap   p pot

r rat   s sat   t top

v vote   w won   x fo**x** e**x**it

y **y**es happ**y** fl**y**   z zip

a ate at   e **fee** n**e**t

i ice r**i**p   o m**o**p b**ow**

u nut cl**ue**

Appendix – D

Helpful Information

Request for Assistance

Although we cannot promise, we will try to help with special situations or questions. We will NOT do this over the telephone. You must e-mail your question to neuro@read.net or send via regular mail to Neuro-Learning Systems, 25725 Long Corner Road, Gaithersburg, Md. 20882. If you send a letter please include a self addressed, stamped envelope. We must also limit this to two questions per person. If we are overwhelmed with requests we retain the right to stop offering this service.

If you ask a question make sure that you include enough information for us to understand your situation. Make sure that you include the student's age, grade, reading level working on and any other information that might be useful.

We always offer a fee based help service. This service is at the rate of $75.00 per hour. We will provide you with an estimate of the cost prior to accepting your request.

Enrollment Application

If you are interested in applying for professional tutoring either in person or over the phone please visit our web site at http://www.neurolearning.net   If you are not familiar with the internet, please write or fax (443-788-2587) us and request an application. Please be advised that we are usually busy and have had waiting lists of over two hundred people. It is impossible to predict what our status will be when you read this book.

From time to time we do have some limited scholarships available. They are for households with gross incomes under forty thousand dollars. They are usually fifty percent or less. If you would like to apply for a scholarship please be aware that you must be willing to release income tax data for us to verify income. Either go to our website at http://neuro.read.net/scholarship.html and use that application or write us for one.

Training Application

We offer training in our method to parents and teachers. Parents do not need an education background. We also offer training for schools. School administrators should contact our office to discuss our training program.

Parents and teachers acting as individuals are offered training at sites around the world. We conduct all day workshops to train individuals to use our program. This training is for classrooms and, it is for one-on-one teaching. Our programs start at 9 a.m. and end at 3 p.m. The tuition per student varies based on the training site. Participants must also purchase this book for the training. Other materials are provided.

Those interested should either request an application via fax (443-788-2587), e-mail or regular mail or go to our website at http://www.neurolearning.net/mdtraining.html and use that application. We usually have a waiting list well into the hundreds. We offer training during the week and on Saturdays. Logging is available at the training site for those traveling from out of state. Logging expenses are extra. We are also available to come to your site if you have a group of twenty or more students. Please contact our office if you have such a group.

Book Order Form

You may order books via the U.S. Mail or over the internet. We DO NOT take book orders over the telephone. Please either go to our internet site at http://www.neuro.read.net/bookorder.html or write us a letter. Mail the letter to Neuro-Learning Systems, 25725 Long Corner Road, Gaithersburg, Md. 20882 . You may also fax to (443-788-2587).

Refer to the book list in Appendix B. Make sure that you list all of the books that you want. There is a $3.90 shipping and handling fee per book set. We do not sell the books at the 4.1 level and above. Book prices are as listed on the internet site http://www.neuro.read.net/bookprice.html If you do not have internet access, please send us a letter requesting prices. We do not accept requests over the telephone. If you live in Maryland you must add sales tax at 5%.

Your order must be paid for before we ship the books. If you pay by check we will wait until the check clears. Add the price of the books, and $3.90 shipping (plus 5% tax if you live in Md.). We will contact you if there is a discrepancy in prices. Prices are subject to change at any time.